MW01002513

EARTHBORN DEMOCRACY

CRITICAL LIFE STUDIES

CRITICAL LIFE STUDIES

Jami Weinstein, Claire Colebrook, and Myra J. Hird, series editors

The core concept of critical life studies strikes at the heart of the dilemma that contemporary critical theory has been circling around: namely, the negotiation of the human, its residues, a priori configurations, the persistence of humanism in structures of thought, and the figure of life as a constitutive focus for ethical, political, ontological, and epistemological questions. Despite attempts to move quickly through humanism (and organicism) to more adequate theoretical concepts, such haste has impeded the analysis of how the humanist concept of life is preconfigured or immanent to the supposedly new conceptual leap. The Critical Life Studies series thus aims to destabilize critical theory's central figure, life—no longer should we rely upon it as the horizon of all constitutive meaning but instead begin with life as the problematic of critical theory and its reconceptualization as the condition of possibility for thought. By reframing the notion of life critically—outside the orbit and primacy of the human and subversive to its organic forms—the series aims to foster a more expansive, less parochial engagement with critical theory.

Edward S. Casey and Michael Marder, *Plants in Place: A Phenomenology of the Vegetal*

Paul B. Preciado, *Countersexual Manifesto*

Vincent Bruyere, *Perishability Fatigue: Forays Into Environmental Loss and Decay*

Penelope Deutscher, *Foucault's Futures: A Critique of Reproductive Reason*

Jami Weinstein and Claire Colebrook, eds., *Posthumous Life: Theorizing Beyond the Posthuman*

Luce Irigaray and Michael Marder, *Through Vegetal Being: Two Philosophical Perspectives*

EARTHBORN DEMOCRACY

A Political Theory of Entangled Life

ALI ASLAM, DAVID W. MCIVOR,
AND JOEL ALDEN SCHLOSSER

Columbia University Press

New York

Columbia University Press
Publishers Since 1893
New York   Chichester, West Sussex
cup.columbia.edu

Library of Congress Cataloging-in-Publication Data

Names: Aslam, Ali, author. | McIvor, David Wallace, author. |
Schlosser, Joel Alden, author.
Title: Earthborn democracy : a political theory of entangled life /
Ali Aslam, David McIvor, and Joel Alden Schlosser.
Description: New York : Columbia University Press, [2024] |
Series: Critical life studies / Jami Weinstein, Claire Colebrook,
and Myra J. Hird, series editors | Includes bibliographical
references and index.
Identifiers: LCCN 2024009374 (print) | LCCN 2024009375
(ebook) | ISBN 9780231216418 (hardback) | ISBN 9780231216425
(trade paperback) | ISBN 9780231561273 (ebook)
Subjects: LCSH: Democracy—Environmental aspects. |
Ecology—Political aspects. | Democracy and environmentalism.
Classification: LCC JA75.8 .A835 2024 (print) | LCC JA75.8
(ebook) | DDC 321.8—dc23/eng/20240316
LC record available at https://lccn.loc.gov/2024009374
LC ebook record available at https://lccn.loc.gov/2024009375

Cover design: Chang Jae Lee
Cover image: © Shutterstock

To all the earthborn(e)

CONTENTS

EARTHBORN DEMOCRACY

INTRODUCTION

EARTHBORN(E) DEMOCRACY

POLITICS IS A MATTER OF STORIES, and stories matter because of myth. Mythmaking nourishes imagination, creativity, and the renewal of meaning for collective life. *Earthborn Democracy* engages in conscious mythmaking about democracy in relationship with ecology, which refuses the very separation of the terms themselves. An earthborn(e) democracy begins from the twinned ideas that democracy is an ecological habitat and that ecological flourishing is democratic. There is no "people" (*demos*) without the earth, and no power (*kratos*) without cooperation between and among different species and systems that constitute the earth. When humans as a species attune to the abundance of democratic possibilities within the history of life on this planet, they find themselves much more resourceful and capable than previously imagined. Anxiety, hopelessness, and fear in this moment of deep uncertainty have spread like a wildfire across the psychosocial landscape.

Myths of earthborn(e) democracy, as well as the stories and rituals consonant with these myths, awaken us to a different situation, one less overwhelmed than empowered and more confident than despairing.

Earthborn Democracy acknowledges such anxieties and the reasons for fear, paralysis, and despair in the contemporary moment of crisis. The seeming prosperity brought about by modern industry and the spread of the carbon-intensive economy has also entailed enormous waste, pollution, and environmental despoliation. Ecological catastrophes and the slow violence of environmental harm—caused largely by human activities and the surrounding fantasies of control, exceptionalism, and supremacy—threaten all forms of life on earth. The threats born of the climate crisis feel even more menacing because of their unpredictability. As the species exits a ten-thousand-year window of relative stability, the only certainty is uncertainty.

Adding to ecological anxieties is the angst over democracy itself. In the era of the planet's sixth mass extinction, democracy, too, may be endangered.[1] There is both decreasing confidence in democratic ideals and a corresponding decline in democratic practices, norms, and institutions. Popular discontent, elite malfeasance, and unresponsive institutions herald democratic crisis, if not collapse. Rising authoritarianism around the world; the closing down of public spaces for contestation of elite rule; the erosion of institutional safeguards; war and conflict; and the atrophy of citizen knowledge, experience, and fitness all point to the dwindling prospects for democracy's survival.

Democracy also suffers a twofold reputational crisis. On the one hand, democracy's association with the modern state's worst offenses—the slave trade, capitalist exploitation, dispossession and genocide of Indigenous populations, and environmental degradation—has so tarnished its reputation that many of today's "freedom dreams" eschew the language of democracy entirely.[2] Liberal democracy has accompanied modern industrial development (and indeed relied on it), and this has meant that democracy is an accomplice to the ecological exploitation upon which such development rests.[3] On the other hand, the urgency of this moment casts democracy in an undesirable light: its requirements of deliberation, participation, and reflective revision make it seem incapable of the immediate and sustained action that ecological crisis demands.[4] Therefore, the twin crises of ecology and democracy impel some to look beyond democracy itself, since democracy seems too limited in both what it promises and delivers.[5]

Democracy, at its core, consists of the aspiration for cooperation across difference in the name of collective freedom. The original meaning of democracy, according to Josiah Ober, is "the capacity of the people to do things together."[6] This capacity is stunted by modern institutions such as elections, which cement a vision of "managed democracy," where the powers of the people are channeled to generate the power upon which the state and global economy depend.[7] Democratic power is extracted through rituals of popular legitimation that reinforce loyalty to the traditions and institutions of the constitutional state. The possibilities of democracy, however, are not fully extinguished by such rituals but persist as aspirations for self-rule and collective freedom. Democracy thrives when the diverse intelligence and genius of ordinary people is liberated and expressed in rituals, institutions, and myths of their own making.

Democracy, on our reading, is not exhausted by its instantiation in liberal-democratic institutions, the settler colonial state, or market economies; the latter trio, indeed, are themselves increasingly inadequate vehicles for addressing present-day crises. We believe, however, that these inadequacies are less about the institutions themselves and are more about symptoms of failing politico-cultural *stories* and a corresponding lack of coherence for the now disparate practices of eco-political renewal. The effects of climate change and ecological disruption, along with the diminished desires for democracy, are the pathological results of inhabiting an anthropocentric myth of control and sovereignty over the earth.

An adequate response to the twin crises of democracy and ecology therefore begins with conscious mythmaking. In this book, we articulate myths of what we call *earthborn(e) democracy*, which reawaken us to the fact that human beings live *in* (and not just *on*) the earth, in entangled, dynamic relations with all other earthly creatures. Being earthborn(e) denotes two overlapping conditions. First, to be earthborn(e) is to be carried and supported by the earth—*borne* by the earth and dependent on its ecological cycles; yet, second, to be earthborn(e) is also to be *born* out of the earth—to be natal, something new and miraculous, an emergent being not previously encountered.[8] To be earthborn(e) is to resonate with the earth, while also being able to draw upon its powers in order to imagine and pursue projects of collective freedom and flourishing. The condition of being earthborn(e) then, is a Janus-faced situation of attunement and emergence. Earthborn(e) democracy calls us to attend to archetypal patterns of action as paths of renewal. Embodying the myths of earthborn(e) democracy involves attuning to deep histories of possibility contained within the earth and the life of the species. Yet this attunement occasions and elicits emergence—new hymns of possibility resonant with the choral echoes of the past.

Myth is lifeless without rituals. *Earthborn Democracy* re-stories democratic rituals by showing how attunement to resonant patterns of earthly life opens up new forms and imaginaries of democratic practice. From within myths of the earthborn(e), these rituals include and involve the more-than-human world. Although democracy emphasizes the role that power (*kratos*) plays in collective life, this power is not an exclusively human possession but an effect of entangled agency among humans, nonhuman species, and the earth.[9] Here we build on insights about the inherent connections between perception, sensual aliveness, agency, and the more-than-human world.[10] These connections have been obscured and damaged by the conditions of modern life,[11] but they remain vital—both as needs to be fulfilled and as bases for further collective development. By "earthly entanglement" we denote the condition of interdependence between human and more-than-human as well as the cocreated nature of power that this entails.[12] Earthborn(e) democracy illuminates political rituals that enflesh the myths of being earthborn(e). Ecology and democracy must be thought and enacted together for each to flourish.

To undertake this work, we situate ourselves in the tradition of political theory. For Sheldon Wolin, political theory as a tradition organizes itself around the concept of the political. But since the "political" is a historically contested idea, political theory involves both continuity of preoccupations and innovation as it faces emergent phenomena. For Wolin, political theory is at its most vital when it comes as a response to crisis or impasse; that is, when the terms and the stories by which collective life has oriented itself decline in their efficacy or lead to dead ends. Political theory, on this reading, is an inherently visionary activity, because it insists that the world as it is does not exhaust the possibilities of what the world might become.[13] Much of contemporary political theory, however, is not positioned to move us beyond impasse, because it sees itself from within the terms of modernity's dominant stories, either as critique, reform, or midwifery of something better.[14] Political theory needs to take a further step—namely, by reappraising the encompassing myths in which these particular stories make sense—to envision myths that can reorient the species toward freedom and flourishing. In this book, we engage in this more radical practice—going deeper and further, into prehistory as well as the collective unconscious. The chapters that follow pursue the work of conscious mythmaking around democracy and ecology, revitalizing an old but ongoing and evergreen story for new possibilities of collective life on earth.

EARTHLY POLITICS

Although a swelling chorus of thinkers in political theory and elsewhere is reconceptualizing the relationship between politics and the earth, few give specific attention to the mythic.[15] Two exceptions to this general trend are Bruno Latour and Donna Haraway, who have both centered storytelling in their eco-theorizing. Latour has argued that an earthly politics adequate to contemporary ecological crises requires a realignment of political stories. On his reading, modern politics has existed along a continuum between what he calls "global" and "local" attractors. The global attractor envisions and holds out the promise of progress as economic, moral, scientific, and political unification against the inertia of traditional lifeways and the recalcitrance of specific differences. The global flattens out differences in the name of a cosmopolitan consciousness, and insofar as politics is shaped by this attractor the local is seen as an archaic inconvenience. The local, however, has its pull, too; for Latour, populisms of left and right envision a politics of belonging and meaning in line with surviving traditions that have more or less successfully resisted the onslaught of capitalist modernity. The local attracts political will because it offers the promise of respite from the unceasing change lionized by the global attractor.

Yet, for Latour, the assumptions of these attractors no longer suffice for political struggle. Neither pole can live up to its self-declared promises; the local cannot protect itself from the global, and the reach of the global is incomplete and patchy. The climate crisis reveals the limits of each pole—a global, unfolding event whose impacts are differential, yet with effects on every corner of the earth. A resident of Miami is in greater potential solidarity with a person in Vanuatu than a resident of North Dakota, yet no existing politico-cultural narrative or institution encapsulates and speaks to this condition.

As the global-local story has broken down, a new attractor has arisen: an "out of this world" attractor, which offers a fantasy of escaping from what Hannah Arendt called the conditions of living on this earth.[16] In this imaginary, the earth is merely a dying rock from which we need to escape as quickly as possible. The goal is to become a multiplanetary species, by doubling down on Promethean myths of mastery and technological advancement. For Latour, this heralds a post-political moment, which denies any common world or ground for political action.[17]

Unless we believe we can escape the conditions of living on earth—a highly dubious proposition—the out-of-this-world attractor requires a contending force, which Latour describes as the "terrestrial." The terrestrial articulates another, more grounded, political imaginary, a geopolitics that takes the earth as an actor, and not merely as scenery or backdrop. According to Latour, the "geo" (earth) in *geopolitics* designates an agent that participates fully in public life.[18] Any policy that does not start from an idea of agency that is distributed not just to humans but also to the more-than-human world misses the earthly entanglement that is now more apparent than ever. The conditions brought to light by the climate crisis show how the terrestrial possesses us more than we possess the terrestrial. For

Latour, the earth is the sovereign and the essential political slogan of the moment is "Toward the Terrestrial!"[19]

Latour proposes a variety of practical possibilities for living out this geopolitical maxim, but the real politics rests at the level of stories. On this point, Latour is aligned with Donna Haraway, who has proliferated stories of multispecies entanglement that could lead to political reimagination. The stories she tells forward the question of what geo-politico-cultural age we currently inhabit. She argues against calling this period by the name Anthropocene, which highlights the human impact on planetary-scale systems, preferring the term "Chthulucene": "Specifically, unlike either the Anthropocene or the Capitalocene, the Chthulucene is made up of ongoing multispecies stories and practices of becoming-with in times that remain at stake, in precarious times, in which the world is not finished and the sky is not fallen—yet. We are at stake to each other . . . human beings are with and of the earth, and the biotic and abiotic powers of this earth are the main story."[20]

The main story is best transmitted and embodied by what Haraway calls carrier bags or "netbags"—"capacious bags for collecting, carrying, and telling the stuff of the living."[21] Haraway elevates Ursula Le Guin (especially the Hainish fabulations) and Octavia Butler (especially her Parable novels) as exemplary storytellers for the Chthulucene. Haraway weaves her own netbag by re-storying humans as compost: as complex sites or processes of mixing, generating, and enriching new life forms that are attuned to their roles in an entangled, interdependent ecosystem.[22]

Haraway's "Camille Stories: Children of Compost" is an account of multigenerational entangled life, in which fugitive human communities resettle in devastated landscapes while the larger urban centers of population steadily dwindle and decline. In these fugitive spaces, humans practice "symbiogenesis," or interspecies kin-making. Human children are symbiotically linked to another species, which overcomes the narrow speciesism prevalent among humans and fosters cross-species identification and solidarity beyond what is currently imaginable. Because the nonhuman partners within the symbiosis are migratory, humans better learn to see themselves as participants within an unfolding process of life, unconstrained by narrow borders of belonging and identity. Stories like these embody the ethos of entanglement, and storytelling itself, for Haraway, is sustenance—as important as food or water.

As the "Camille Stories" illustrates, Haraway's account of creative storytelling adequate for the Chthulucene emphasizes multispecies cooperation and mutualism, which she notes contrasts with the need for enemies that Latour's earth sovereignty implies.[23] Latour, Haraway writes, pits "humans" against the "earthbound,"[24] which replays the famous (and problematic) distinction between friend and enemy as the basic political question formulated by Carl Schmitt. "Latour's Gaia stories deserve better companions in storytelling than Schmitt," writes Haraway.[25] Tentacular netbag stories like the "Camille Stories" illustrate transformative practices that "are [of] little use in trials of strength but of great use in bringing home and sharing the means of living and dying well, perhaps even a means of ecological recuperation for human and more-than-human critters alike."[26]

While Latour and Haraway call attention to the importance of stories for earthly politics, their stories of multispecies
entanglement and cooperation understate the imbrication of
the twin crises of ecology and democracy. Although their stories of entanglement eloquently and accurately describe the
world we've entered in the Anthropocene/Chthulucene, they
do not by themselves suggest how this entanglement must come
to affect political rituals and institutions (and vice versa)—how
such entanglement must be lived, collectively, going forward.[27]
Myths of earthborn(e) democracy hold together stories, ideas,
or practices for how the human species can democratically "go
on together" in the midst of earthly entanglement.[28] For instance,
Latour figures the earth as a reactive sovereign in a way that
simply shifts sovereignty as a mode of action from the modern nation-state to the earth. This implicit Hobbesianism
precludes the possibility of mutuality or attuned interaction;
it is hard to imagine reciprocity among humans and the terrestrial under the conditions of the state of war that Latour
envisions. Additionally, Haraway invokes the Haudenosaunee Confederacy, but only to note its longitudinal commitment to the seventh generation, overlooking its history of
democratic rituals and institutions. Haraway's all too brief
glance at the experience of the Haudenosaunee leaves open
the possibility of linking stories of the earthborn(e) to a democratic politics of world-making. The future of the earth and
of democracy in it depends upon stories drawn from deep
histories both material and psychic that trace pathways of
entanglement and inspire cooperative action toward earthly
flourishing.[29]

THE EARTHBORN(E) DEMOS

One of the misleading myths of modernity is that democracy is a product of the eighteenth century, and that it is thereby necessarily housed in the nation-state, bounded by a constitution, and embodied by liberal-democratic norms and rituals.[30] This modern myth represses an unruly and wild history of democratic practices stretching across time and space, beyond the ancient Athenian democracy so feared by the American founders.[31] As illustrated by David Graeber (among others), democratic practices are not a modern invention; they have existed under many different titles and within many different traditions—sharing features like popular assemblies and consensus decision-making—across a long arc of human history. The deep history of democratic ideas and practices has been made fugitive, in the language of Sheldon Wolin, by the rise of constitutional democracy and the nation-state, which have sought to contain democracy in ways that vitiate its energies and compromise its potential reach into everyday life. From the perspective of the modern state, the demos must be managed, regulated, and controlled, and subsumed to the seemingly "nonpolitical" directives of the economy and economic growth. Yet this story truncates, if not represses, the deeper history of democracy, which we argue—if adequately recovered—can serve as a repository for reimagining the possibilities of collective life in a time of crisis.[32]

For both better and worse, ancient Athens has been a reference point for so-called Western democratic imagination and praxis. Whether seen as a cautionary tale or as an inspiring exemplar, Athens serves as a distant mirror for fantasies, fears, and hopes with respect to democracy. We maintain that there is an overlooked aspect of the Athenian experience that is relevant to the entangled crises of ecology and democracy—namely, the Greek myth of autochthony, or the idea that the members of the political community were "earth-born."[33] The term "earth-born," while widespread in the ancient Hellenic world (and beyond), is widely associated with and known through the Athenian democracy. The myth of autochthony is rarely mentioned by those who seek inspiration in the Athenian polis,[34] but on our reading it can serve as a reminder of earthly entanglement and as the basis for a re-storying and re-mythologizing of democracy on the earth.[35]

The language of being earthborn is double-sided. Autochthony was often used as a basis of exclusion, or of policing the boundaries of membership within the polis.[36] For example, Pericles's citizenship laws of 451/0 BCE formalized autochthony to limit political membership to those with two "native-born" parents.[37] To be autochthonous in this sense was to be able to trace one's ancestry into a time immemorial or to be able to show continued inhabitation of the same territory within one's lineage. In this instance the autochthony myth was deployed as a justification for discrimination. Pericles's laws constituted a particular political interpretation of the myth, but autochthony did not only afford this more restrictive deployment.[38] Autochthony was also used to radically expand membership within the polis. The story of Erechtheus, the founder of Athens who was "born of the earth," came to color *autochthon* such that autochthony denoted not just continuous inhabitation but also being earthborn.[39] Autochthony here includes all beings that come from the earth. Although the myth of autochthony is often interpreted as supporting an exclusionary nationalism or nativism, a crucial moment in the emergence of Athenian democracy suggests how the myth was also deployed in an inclusionary direction. According to Aristotle's *Constitution of Athens*, in the late sixth century, Kleisthenes enfranchised a significant number of non-Athenians, declaring them autochthonous. Autochthony here was used to signify inclusion on the basis of common connection to the land in resistance to political norms of exclusion.

Autochthony also heralded a vision of distributed agency among humans and the more-than-human world. Being born of the earth also included "insignificant creatures" like mice,[40] an expansiveness that angered critics concerned with drawing clear lines among human communities. Even though autochthony was used for political purposes to draw boundaries, then, the broader mythical and earthly resonances extending to the more-than-human were never fully absent. Comic and tragic poets, orators, and philosophers played with telling and retelling stories of being earthborn to a variety of ends. The fifth-century comic poet Poliochus jokes about autochthonous vegetables—locally cultivated and yet still wild—showing the different ways the concept was taken up.[41]

Acknowledging these different deployments of autochthony and their varied political consequences, then, we propose taking "autochthonous" not simply as a discursive space for contesting political boundary-drawing, but as reflecting a deeper reality of earthly entanglement; the Athenian democracy carries traces of earthborn(e) democracy. Myths of earthborn(e) democracy, as discussed above, insist that the demos consists of all creatures born of the earth—both human and nonhuman.[42] These creatures share the status of being born of and borne by the earth as described above: they emerge from the earth and are carried or sustained by it. In both senses, power is an earthly phenomenon: the earth gives birth to earthly creatures whose lives depend on it. Being earthborn(e) denotes an earthly mutualism and interdependence: all earthly creatures are conditioned by living *in* the earth.

Interpreters of autochthony often focus on the politics of inclusion and exclusion within the category of the human, but they miss the constitutive exclusion of the nonhuman within their own interpretive assumptions. The story of autochthony offers more than a metaphor for earthly entanglement but, rather, a substantial vision for what all earthborn beings have in common. Earthborn(e) democracy begins from the earthly mutualism and cooperation that this entails. Contrary to Carl Schmitt's vision in *The* Nomos *of the Earth*, where humans remain the only relevant actors and politics rests upon the basic distinction of friend-enemy, the *nomoi* of earthborn(e) democracy arise in responsive interactions among human and nonhuman.[43] In his critical engagement with Schmitt, Latour approaches this idea of the earthborn(e), yet his political imaginary is still saturated with a Hobbesian logic of sovereignty that belies the messy and radical entanglement that the democratic dimension of earthborn(e) democracy engages.[44]

Focusing on the narrow, political uses of autochthony in ancient Athens, interpreters of the myth have also largely missed an opportunity to connect the Athenian story with other Indigenous and non-Western practices of democracy. Yet exploring such connections reveals the continuous recurrence of democratic experience and aspiration across time and space. Drawing linkages between historically and culturally disparate political communities expands the democratic archive by illustrating earthly rituals and repertoires; this can, in turn, embolden and encourage democratic experimentation beyond the narrow liberal-democratic imaginary of the last 250 years.

Pulling back the lens on democracy and ecology broadens the perspective in ways that recontextualize feelings of impasse or "stuckness." Far from being an affective dead end, as Gloria Anzaldúa argues, impasse is a sign of and incitement to emergence, creativity, and cooperative action. What Anzaldúa calls spiritual activism is also rooted in a sense of being earthborn(e), of being carried and sustained by the earth in ways that inspire acts of renewal and restoration.[45] Similarly, Robin Wall Kimmerer, a member of the Potawatomi nation and trained biologist, helps to connect the story of autochthony to Indigenous epistemologies and practices when she suggests how settler communities can nevertheless become "Indigenous to place."[46] "To be Indigenous," Kimmerer writes, "is to protect life on earth."[47] The myth of autochthony, we suggest, can function like what Kimmerer refers to as "Original Instructions," which provide an orientation but not a map for earthly flourishing.[48] For instance, prescriptions for respectful hunting, based on consensual relations with the more-than-human, are understood both as a means of ensuring human flourishing and as a way of responding to and respecting interdependence with the earth and its other creatures. The Original Instructions might be available to descendants of settler colonists, if not for the repression of being earthborn(e) that went hand in glove with the violent suppression of Indigenous peoples.[49]

Along with Indigenous accounts of the Original Instructions, the myth of autochthony can offer guidance for a democratic politics under conditions of earthly entanglement. An expansive myth of autochthony also prefigures an alternative to the reactive sovereignty of Latour's political vision, and it reconnects Haraway's netbags to the democratic work of worldmaking. Like Anzaldúa's spiritual activism, the myth of autochthony centers the movement away from impasse and onto the renewal that comes from attunement to sources of nurturance beyond the here and now. The political flexibility of the myth, moreover, supports the process of becoming Indigenous to place, which is a central challenge for ecological democracy in this critical moment.

VISIONARY POLITICAL THEORY

Earthborn Democracy embodies what we refer to as visionary political theory. Taking our cue once again from Sheldon Wolin, we understand vision in two senses: first, as a commitment to perceive political realities for what they are; and, second, as an imaginative, aesthetic, and even fanciful endeavor irreducible to those realities. Vision is about seeing clearly the world as it is while also seeing creatively in ways that attune perception to possibilities for emergence and transformation. Wolin argues that political theory turns on the work of imagination to fill in the gaps between experience of the world and desire for what it might become.[50] Visionary political theory on our argument elaborates Wolin's twofold account of vision and reflects while amplifying practices of renewal, restoration, and resonance that are essential to the myths of earthborn(e) democracy.[51]

Visionary political theory involves a new way of looking at the familiar world. Historically, political theory has been characterized by architectonic impulses to alter and control the world. Yet visionary political theory balances the heroic (masculine) mode in which theory has often been conducted through the work of attunement and tending, as opposed to the aspirations for mastery of political phenomena. Tending by contrast attempts to encourage and amplify emergent possibilities.[52] Visionary political theory shares the long-standing concern within political theory for confronting contemporary crises— for tracing the dark edges of unfreedom and the possibilities for catastrophe. Yet visionary political theory is equally committed to the possibilities of renewal in the face of danger, despair, and impasse. "Evening" philosophy requires an anticipation of daybreak.[53] Last, like much of contemporary political theory, visionary theory is concerned with attending to the values and ideals at stake in political contestation, defending these against a critical skepticism that denies any possibility for a just political order.[54] At the same time, visionary theory calls into question existing practices and institutions through its commitment to a deeper level of analysis that acknowledges how all norms and values are shadowed by structures that can compromise or even make a mockery of those values.[55]

Visionary political theory shapes the approach of *Earthborn Democracy*. Vision is what allows us to create and revise images of the self—individual and collective—and attune to fields or repertoires of creativity and imagination that resonate across space and time and provide resources for responding to crisis and impasse. Vision motivates the work of gathering and studying ignored archives of political theory and praxis; it encourages immersion into the realms of mythology and the collective unconscious; and it seeks out ways of embodying and practicing political ideals as rituals of democratic life.[56] Visionary political theory is an imaginative account of restoration—of how collective life organizes and orients itself as well as how it might do otherwise. Any new organization requires re-storying of the constitutive myths of collective life, with restoration as both return and initiation. Myth depends upon ritual to instantiate collective life. Above (or below) all, the visionary theory on offer here is a theory of the earthborn(e); it reorients political inquiry and practice to the double nature of being borne by the earth and emerging or being born from it. The condition of being earthborn(e) is the means of both accurately perceiving earthly realities and generating imaginative possibilities for flourishing and freedom amid earthly entanglement.

We develop this theory of earthborn(e) democracy in three chapters. In the first chapter, we upend the conventional historical account of democracy centered on ancient Athens by retelling deep histories of egalitarian political organization from the premodern Americas to Mesopotamia and beyond.

Examining recent findings in archaeology and anthropology, we identify practices of democracy that are more playful, egalitarian, and attuned to place and the more-than-human than modern, hierarchically organized state-based forms. We expand the archive of democracy's existence in "surprising" contexts that have, until now, been overlooked and even denied by scholars who believe that democratic aspirations are bound to the modern nation-state system. We highlight elements of earthly- and species-entanglement at the heart of these examples and amplify the resonances of these historical episodes with the epistemologies and lifeways of extant Indigenous communities in North America. This prompts reconsideration of the origins of democracy in Athens and its myth of autochthony, re-storying the birth of democracy as a more expansive, inclusive story of continual rebirth and renewal through practices of multispecies cooperation.

In the second chapter, we turn to depth psychology to explore and develop an understanding of myth as the necessary substratum of political life. From this vantage point, we develop a notion of the earthborn(e) unconscious and we give a democratic rereading of the Jungian archetypes, which we suggest organize aspirations for democratic and ecological forms of life. The archetypes and the collective unconscious are a species inheritance that serve as an available reservoir for nourishing political imagination and praxis. We identify three democratic archetypes—of flight, sociality, and politicality—that reappear across the long arc of human (and more-than-human) histories. The archetypes are reminders of chthonic roots, and they situate the repertoires and range of tools for confronting threats to earthly flourishing.

Chapter 3 takes up, elaborates, and complicates the myths of earthborn(e) democracy through democratic rituals of earthly entanglement. We turn to Leanne Betasamosake Simpson's Nishnaabeg resurgence, Cooperation Jackson's proliferation of cooperative structures and economic democracy, and broadbased organizing's relational power building to show how seemingly disparate examples ranging across cultural communities that are differently positioned within settler colonialism appear consonant with one another in light of myths of earthborn(e) democracy. Positioned in a theory of ritual as the dynamic interrelation between attunement and emergence, these democratic practices enflesh earthborn(e) democracy, both illustrating its possible forms and suggesting how other distinctive rituals might emerge in different contexts. All these examples and the relationships between them become more intelligible through the account of democratic archetypes developed in chapter 2 and myths of earthborn(e) democracy elaborated in chapter 1. These rituals of entangled agency open new pathways and patterns for less exploitative and extractive forms of collective life.

In this moment of twinned crises—where both earthly life and democracy seem to hang in the balance—earthborn(e) democracy surfaces long-buried stories of collective freedom and flourishing rooted in earthly attachment and belonging. In doing so, it re-stories democratic life in ways that resonate with the deep history of the species. Multispecies cooperation is an earthly inheritance, and it represents an ever-present possibility for renewal. Our earthly or chthonic origins are the starting point for imagining and instantiating democratic flourishing. Remythologizing these chthonic origins allows for the envisioning and eliciting of new political futures, which emerge from the depths of earthly life. This life is not merely chronicled in the known history of the species but also held in the collective unconscious, which spans culture, time, and place. Attunement through the stories of earthborn(e) democracy opens the space for rituals of democratic self-fashioning amid earthly entanglement and distributed agency. *Earthborn Democracy* insists on conscious mythmaking surrounding the intertwined fates of ecology and democracy, showing how each is a necessary companion for the other if life on earth is to have its future.

Chapter One

PATHS NOT TAKEN

RESONANT HISTORIES OF
EARTHBORN(E) DEMOCRACY

*Social science has largely been a study of the way that
human beings are not free. . . . What is the purpose of all
this . . . knowledge if not to reshape our conceptions of
who we are and what we are yet to become?*
—David Graeber and David Wengrow, *The Dawn of Everything*

*We are dreaming of a time when the land might give
thanks for the people.*
—Robin Wall Kimmerer, *Braiding Sweetgrass*

IN THIS FLUID MOMENT of crisis and catastrophe, it's an open
question as to which will die off first, the human species,
democracy, or the ecosystems supporting life as we know it. The
so-called crisis of democracy obscures the real problem: it's not
just that democracy is in crisis, subject to decline, deficits, or
"backsliding." The crisis of democracy is such that what goes
by the name of democracy is a hollow shell, a rhetorical entomb-
ing, of a vibrant form of collective flourishing on the earth.
The democracy crisis is interwoven with (and exacerbated by)
the ecological crisis, as well as the many facets of out-of-joint

relationships between the human and more-than- human world. While some use the urgency of the climate crisis to argue for non- or anti-democratic solutions, pitting democracy against ecology, we want to argue for their mutual intertwinement.

In this chapter, we begin by deepening the history of democracy, tracing the aspirations and practices associated with collective self-governance far beyond the relatively narrow historical imaginaries of political theory and contemporary social science. Through this inquiry, we argue that the visions of how democratic forms of life can honor and attune to earthly entanglements are both very old and evergreen. Nevertheless, these visions have been denied, disavowed, or repressed for nearly as long as they have persisted. Sheldon Wolin coined the term "fugitive democracy" to describe how robust visions and practices of democratic life have always been endangered, in part due to tendencies toward institutionalization.[1] Wolin insists that democracy cannot exist in a permanent form: "democracy" fitted to constitutional institutions inevitably suffocates. Institutionalization marks the attenuation of democracy—leaders, hierarchies, and experts as well as order, procedure, and precedent all displace a more spontaneous and relational politics of collective self-governance. The settled practices of institutionalization are joined by routinization and standardization that diminish the improvisatory enactments characteristic of democracy.

The formal functions of the state all conspire against the demos. The state is predicated on a way of viewing the world ("seeing like a state," in James C. Scott's evocative phrase),[2] which emphasizes the inevitability of hierarchy, representation, and the need for management and control over populations, security, territory, economy, and environment.³ This way of viewing the world is a significant dimension of the unspoken myth of modernity, in which democracy is imprisoned. Modernity's myth does not understand itself as myth but as myth's replacement. Yet it serves a mythic function in organizing and justifying existing forms of life, while painting alternatives as unrealistic, unviable, and undesirable. Modern rationalism and realism masquerade as mythless, but this reinforces a dogma of human omnipotence expressed as the desire to reshape and control the human and more-than-human worlds. Such a mythology has displaced the idea of power as a means to repair the world and replaced it with power as domination over earth and other humans. The effects of this are to obscure the periodicity of life, separate humans from the rhythms and limits of nature, and alienate humans from the ways in which those limits can and must shape the exercise of power.

Readers of Wolin take his analysis of fugitive democracy as a sober, if not pessimistic, assessment of the possibilities for democracy: that it is doomed or not up to the task of self-governance in the contemporary age. Fugitive democracy is thus read as a counsel of despair.⁴ However, if democracy is fated to evanescence, then what explains the persistent reappearance of democratic aspiration? Why have the ideals of democracy survived in the inhospitable environment of modern myth? In this chapter we begin from the observation that even at moments of apparent resignation to democracy's inadequacy, a collective yearning for democratic praxis endures. As Wolin writes, "The ideal of re-democratization is not dead. It forms part of a recurrent aspiration: to find room in which people can join freely with others to take responsibility for solving their common problems and thereby sharing the modest fate that is the lot of all mortals."[5] Democracy requires a habitat—a holding environment wherein democracy can safely develop[6]—in which the responsibilities of collective life can be expressed, shared, and enjoyed.[7] On our reading, going beyond what Wolin claims, the shrinking of democratic aspiration in modernity is an *environmental* problem, occasioned by a loss or lack of habitat for the expression of the human species' capacity to govern itself in conscious, reciprocal entanglement with the more-than-human world.

In what follows, we offer a concept of earthborn(e) democracy that contextualizes this recurrent aspiration and counters the modern myths of omnipotence over the earth. The earthborn(e) nature of this concept also gives democracy a deeper and more expansive history from which to imagine and instantiate more democratic futures. Such a deep history of democracy contradicts the counsel of despair by indicating the persistence of democratic innovation and desire across space and time. We expand the field of examples of democracy by turning to evidence in contemporary archaeology as well as historical and extant Indigenous thought and praxis. Earthborn(e) democracy builds on Wolin's account of collective self-governance— "to find room in which people can join freely with others to take responsibility for solving their common problems"—and re-envisions it in terms of multispecies entanglements of all earthborn(e) creatures. One strong claim of this book is that there is no democratic flourishing that is not also ecological flourishing, and vice versa. Myths of earthborn(e) democracy attune us to this interrelationship.

Myth always holds a vision of how human and more-than-human worlds live together. All myths are earthborn(e) in this sense, elaborating the normative relationships between earthly beings. Even the modern myth does this: human beings, ideally, control "nature" and all nonhumans with it. The modern myth of "man versus nature" is thus still earthborn(e), just in a self-destructive fashion. While modern mythlessness sets up a contradiction between storytelling and scientific knowledge, we maintain their coexistence. To demonstrate this, we begin this chapter by introducing the theory of morphic resonance, which helps to explain how the aspiration for democracy can and does recur across distant spaces and times, and how it positions us to see democratic capacities as a species inheritance and part of what it means to live a flourishing, earthly life. We then turn to the work of David Graeber and David Wengrow to elaborate a deep history of democratic self-governance that is obscured by the terms of modern myth. While Graeber and Wengrow's contribution to reimagining democracy is paradigm shattering, it has certain silences that we address by turning to extant Indigenous cosmologies and lifeways that emphasize earthly entanglement and the necessary mediation between the visible and invisible. With this more capacious archive in hand, we restory the fugitivity of democracy not as a sign of its evanescence but rather as a sign of persistent democratic hopes, desires, and dreams. These aspirations form a democratic resonance pattern across earthly history, a species inheritance that will only disappear with the elimination of planetary life.

Myth is not optional. It holds the stories we live by and the theories by which we take our bearings. Democratic life—as we saw in the case of the Athenian myth of autochthony in the introduction—requires myth to flourish. Modernity, despite disavowing its mythic character, still creates myths to story and orient human life, but it does so in an anthropocentric manner that hurtles toward ecocide. Politics is not merely a struggle over policy or party, but a struggle over the stories that guide us. This chapter offers an alternative to the mythologies of the modern state, which inhibit democratic flourishing. We need an alternative because these myths are failing: they only offer a vision of human freedom underpinned by destructive patterns of domination of the earth, of both its human and nonhuman inhabitants. Here we argue, on a rereading of the deep history of the species, for a myth of earthborn(e) democracy: a story to bear a democracy born *of* the earth and borne *by* the earth, one in which human and nonhuman freedoms realize themselves in fractious arrays of earthly flourishing.

DEMOCRACY AND MORPHIC RESONANCE

How can we speak constructively of the relationship between democratic aspirations and the deep history of the species? What could give confidence that these histories can speak to moderns, in particular moderns trapped in myths of their own mythlessness? Any myth to support democratic futures needs to account for how moments of fugitive democracy distant across space and time might shape and be shaped by one another.

Our wager is that the persistence of democracy as a form depends upon some transmission among these moments.

The theory of morphic resonance offers a powerful way to describe and explain continuity amid discontinuity. The recurrent aspiration for democracy, we suggest and develop here, can be fruitfully interpreted by light of the theory of morphic resonance. First articulated over a century ago, the theory of morphic resonance explains how the present is informed by the past—and the shapes and forms that the present takes—along with the logic and interplay between stability and creativity.[8] Morphic resonance helps us to see how democratic capacities are part of the collective life of the species that influence present political life in conscious and unconscious ways; this influence can be realized and expanded upon through practices or rituals of attunement.

At the foundation of the theory of morphic resonance is an account of "morphic fields." Fields are "non-material regions of influence extending in space and continuing in time."[9] As defined by Rupert Sheldrake: "[Morphic fields] are localized within and around the systems they organize. . . . They are potential organizing patterns of influence and can appear again physically in other times and places wherever and whenever the physical conditions are appropriate. When they do so, they contain within themselves a memory of their previous physical existences. The process by which the past becomes present within morphic fields is called *morphic resonance*."[10]

There are a few key aspects to this theory of morphic resonance. First, there is a memory in nature: morphic fields hold the forms through which all life evolves. Second, fields become material through canalized pathways of development that are informed by morphic fields. Third, this form-giving happens in the interface of the material and immaterial. Fourth, fields provide a basis for regenesis, imparting form to enable adaptation and renewal.

The theory of morphic resonance is controversial. By seeking immaterial explanations for events and phenomena currently explained through material or mechanical causes, the theory can look like mysticism. One implication of morphic resonance, for instance, is the idea of action at a distance: that looking at somebody can alert that person to turn around, or that before you pick up the phone you might know who's calling by sensing the intention of the caller. Without judging the scientific case one way or another, we use the theory of morphic resonance as a potent vocabulary that provides a clear account of the relationship between the past and the present—at the level of form— that explains and helps us interpret the recurrent aspiration for democracy across discontinuities of time, space, and culture. Moreover (and despite these controversies), the theory of morphic resonance illustrates the resistance of the scientific enterprise to revise its most basic commitments. We make a parallel move here with respect to political theory's relationship to democracy.

In his explanation of morphic fields, Rupert Sheldrake recounts a startling experiment that illustrates the theory of morphic fields. In an experiment at Harvard University, rats bred under laboratory conditions for generations were tasked with escaping from a water maze. In the experiment, rats had to swim to one of two pathways that led out of the water. The wrong path was brightly illuminated while the right one was not. If the rats left on the wrong pathway, they received an electrical shock. During the experiment the two pathways were varied: left became right and right became wrong, as it were. The reduction in the number of errors made by rats was taken as an indication of cumulative learning.

The researchers were interested in testing whether genetic inheritance could influence the success rate of subsequent generations of rats. To evaluate this, rats were bred randomly in each successive generation. Across 32 generations and 15 years, the results disconfirmed an inherited-traits (Lamarckian) theory because over generations rats learned the right pathway more quickly, regardless of whether or not the younger generations were direct descendants of the successful rats of previous generations. In other words, cumulative learning occurred across generations without genetic transmission. Collectively, the rats improved their performance in the test over time. The average number of errors went from over 56 in the first eight generations to 41, 29, and 20 in the second, third, and fourth quartiles of eight generations. The differences among the rats even manifested behaviorally, as later generations appeared more cautious and tentative.

This experiment could be taken to support the theory of morphic fields by providing evidence of species learning without genetic transmission of learning across generations. But further, this species memory is not limited to a particular population in Cambridge, Massachusetts. The learning went beyond the exposed population; the lesson is instead embedded in a morphic field and later generations of a species have access to that field. In the case of the original experiment at Harvard, subsequent experiments showed that rats located elsewhere (and not exposed to rats in the original study) picked up where the Harvard rats left off. What appeared to happen is that the *species* learned something, and that this lesson was available to other members of the species across time and space—a startling finding that flies in face of mechanistic, material theories of learning, or the transmission of species traits.

In other words, according to the theory of morphic fields, shared experiences and lessons for each species are held within a collective, immaterial field. Collective learning across different populations within the same species is not limited to Harvard rats. Rupert Sheldrake also gives the example of IQ tests. The psychologist James Flynn first detected that IQ scores have improved over time: average scores among military recruits have gone from 75 in 1918 to 100 in 1990. This cannot be explained by improvements in education or exposure to television (because the scores began rising prior to television's invention). Flynn himself described this effect as "baffling" but, as Sheldrake suggests it, morphic resonance provides a natural explanation.[11] The cumulative-species exposure to these tests improves the collective ability to perform well on them.

These fields can also organize behavior within species. Take the peloton among professional cyclists. Over a hundred cyclists a few millimeters from one another move together in a tight group at high speeds. They have to respond and react much more quickly than cognition would allow. This is human swarming.[12] The ability to swarm effectively depends on learning to attune to the field, a skill potentially developed through experience but not reducible to experience. Attunement is developed through morphic fields, but we are suggesting that senses of attunement can be sharpened through intentional practice.

Morphic fields are expressed through pathways of development, which Sheldrake names *chreodes*, coming from ancient Greek *chrē* meaning necessary and *hodos* meaning path. It is "a canalized pathway of change within a morphic field."[13] Chreodes stabilize behavior; they are another way to describe habitual action, yet habits are not limited to human beings. The specific chreodes of a field give form to the behavior of minerals, plants, insects, and other animals. The chreode describes the necessary path of formal development, for example the habitual patterns of crystal formation in nature or the shapes of wasp nests.

Fields provide a nonphysical causal factor, the immaterial basis for material expression. Chreodes are the material, embodied habituation of a pathway of development in*formed* by that field. Chreodes tend towards stabilization through iteration, but they also evolve. When environmental requirements allow for repetition, chreodes stabilize; when environmental conditions obstruct repetition, chreodes evolve or shift. The immaterial field is what explains the capacity for adaptation or renewal. Morphic fields persist, but they also change across time through the interface of the material and immaterial. According to Sheldrake, "There is a two-way flow of influence: from fields to organisms and from organisms to fields."[14] When rats learn a new trick (material), it alters the field (immaterial); after this field is altered, rats know the trick without having to "learn" it. The actions of individuals alter the field (provided there are enough individuals).

To put this in the language of democratic theory, we posit a democratic resonance field that is not limited to the present moment, and which exists as an inheritance of the species activity of collective self-governance. The recurrent aspiration for democracy transpires through chreodes that political actors take up, iterate, and lay down. Any iteration depends on how agents embody or act out the inheritance; the field holds forms—it *in*forms—for these activities and the activities elaborate or develop what the field holds. Potential is latent until actualized, but actualization does not exhaust potentiality—at least for a while; potentiality for species learning can diminish over time through an absence of active instantiation or the destruction of a holding environment for these activities. The deep archive developed in this chapter retells histories of collective self-governance that have resonated and hold potential to continue to resonate. These are the resonant histories of earthborn(e) democracy.

The theory of morphic resonance largely fell out of favor in the mid-twentieth century, with significant costs for understanding ecological entanglement, species learning, the collective unconscious, and the importance of rituals. Morphic fields enjoyed their heyday in the early decades of the twentieth century, but they were challenged and displaced by genetic accounts of inheritance that promised a more measurable, material basis for explaining life and its evolution. Genetic accounts of generation and regeneration, however, reduce transmission to direct inheritance, emphasizing commonalities amongst only genetically related individuals. This individualizing, materialist bias overlooks common patterns among both nonrelated and geographically distant members of a single species. The ortho-doxy in this field has closed the door on a certain way of know-ing, but the orthodox view persists in part because it embodies the modern myth of human omnipotence and the species' capacity for manipulating the more-than-human world, which is seen as mute matter ripe for reshaping according to human desires.[15]

Applying the concept of morphic fields to the study of democracy expands the sites and persistence of democratic experience beyond a narrow set of familiar terms. These terms constellate democracy in settled, agricultural patterns of human inhabitation, cities, constitutional forms, and permanent insti-tutions. In contrast to the conventional study of democracy, we suggest that the recurrent aspiration for democracy exists in a morphic field.[16] The morphic field persists through freedom dreams and is embodied or made real through rituals of demo-cratic self-governance across the long stretch of the species' (still fully unwritten) history.[17]

Our concept of democratic morphic field bears similarities to William Connolly's understanding of resonance in his the-ory of "resonance machines." Connolly's theory explores the relationship between body, brain, and culture—how ideas, eth-ical sensibilities, bodily and neurocognitive processes, and social movements all resonate with one another rather than being derivable from a single cause. In articulating this theory, Connolly draws from neuroscientists like Francisco Varela and Antonio Damasio as well as philosophers like Friedrich Nietzsche and Gilles Deleuze. First formulated to describe how American Christianity and "cowboy capitalism" resonate with each other to produce effects that cannot be fully explained through causal accounts, ideological analysis, or interest-group pluralism, "resonance" describes the mixture of two bodies that are "folded, bended, blended, emulsified, and resolved incompletely"—constituting frames, perceptions, and affects thus spread through a kind of social contagion.[18] Connolly's diagnosis also leads to a prescription. To challenge the evangelical/neoliberal resonance machine, counter-resonance machines, produced through the conjoining of disparate movements, must emerge.[19]

These similarities notwithstanding, our emphasis on resonance as a dimension of a theory of morphic fields foregrounds the presence of the past, not merely the emergent dynamics of the current moment. The morphic field of democracy holds a variety of forms—which we detail much more below—that Connolly's resonance machines do not address. We agree with Connolly that the future is not entirely implicit in the past, but we also assert the past holds the possibilities that the future might manifest. Thus we explore the resonance of depths and not just contemporaneous swarms. Connolly's theory of resonance opens the door to this exploration. The morphic field is like the rhizome from which manifold futures blossom and die, and blossom and die.

Overlooking the full morphic field of democracy comes with a cost. Only through attuning to the resonance fields of democratic aspiration can we realize our species inheritance as self-governing beings entangled in the more-than-human world. Connolly approaches the possibility of earthly flourishing with his concept of "vitality," which he describes as acknowledgement and participation in entangled systems, human and more-than-human. Yet this vitality has no resonance across time. Contrary to Connolly's insistence that "the world is not preorganized for us," the theory of morphic resonance shows how prior organization manifests as collective lessons held by an immaterial field or memory of the species.[20] Earthly flourishing comes by attuning to these lessons, not just by responding to emergent conditions but by building from the best of what we as human beings—spread across space and time—have learned to be able to do. To get out of the fucking maze! The task now is to expand our awareness of the breadth and depth of this field, which we do by turning to the work of David Graeber and David Wengrow.

RESONANT HISTORIES
AND DEMOCRATIC MYTHS

According to Graeber and Wengrow, the dominant myth of anthropology is an unexamined orthodoxy that premodern people living without settled agriculture were stupid, violent, and chaotic. One effect of this myth is a bifurcation of political imagination: groups are thought to be either organized and settled or simple and primitive. Anthropology has also conspired with settler colonialism, with its findings serving to justify dogmas of terra nullius, expropriation of land, and domination of so-called primitive peoples. Moreover, because of these beliefs, anthropologists and social scientists at large cannot adequately countenance what Graeber and Wengrow call "the Indigenous critique," a sophisticated and creative refusal to accept the terms of the settler colonial social contract. According to modern assumptions, the Indigenous critique is nothing more than an impotent anachronism—or a romantic fantasy. There can be no comparisons across the divisions erected between civilized and barbarian, settled and unsettled. Anthropological orthodoxies police human knowledge and thereby limit access to the broader field of human experience. Any robust desire for the freedom of an unsettled collective life, untrammeled by hierarchy or bureaucracy or the state, is dismissed as childish and anachronistic, a delusion that denies the inevitability of complex, agriculturally based societies and their encompassing institutions. For Graeber and Wengrow, however, the Indigenous critique is not limited to a particular time and place, but is a live possibility across historical epochs because it represents enduring aspirations for genuinely free forms of life.[21] We could live otherwise, and "even now the possibilities for human intervention are far greater than we are inclined to think" (524).

Graeber and Wengrow's work has two basic moves important for our purposes. First, it shows how the modern story of species evolution is complicated by episodes of discontinuity and deviation, featuring long-existing civilizations characterized by mobility and equality that belie this simple narrative. Building on but going far beyond Murray Bookchin's depiction of an "ecology of freedom,"[22] Graeber and Wengrow describe a kind of "ecological flexibility" illustrated by examples such as "play farming" in Amazonia and elsewhere that unfolded over thousands of years: "The proclivity of human societies to move (freely) in and out of farm; to farm without becoming full

farmers; raise crops and animals without surrendering too
much of one's existence to the logistical rigors of agriculture,
and retain a food web sufficiently broad as to prevent cultivation from becoming a matter of life and death" (260). Inhabitants possessed all the requisite skills and knowledge to raise
crops and livestock but chose to maintain a balance between
forager (or forester) and farmer (268). In Mexico, the Eastern
Woodlands of North America, and China, long gaps between
the capacity to farm and the reliance on farming appear in the
archaeological record (270). The "elaborate and unpredictable
subsistence routines" these arrangements afforded gave groups
the means for maintaining freedom from centralized authorities and their powers of taxation, regulation, and conscrip-
tion (271).[23]

Nebelivka, a prehistoric "mega-site" in the Ukrainian forest-
steppe, provides an example of a civilization characterized by
equality without a hierarchical state. For over eight centuries,
little evidence for warfare or the rise of social elites in Nebelivka arises in the archaeological record. Instead, Nebelivka
appeared to have robust processes for collective decision-
making; inhabitants shared a framework for the settlement as
a whole, a framework based on the image of the circle that was
reflected in the layout of the settlement. For Graeber and Wengrow, the circle symbolizes commitments to equality as well as
the cyclical nature of life and renewal. Similarly, modern Basque
settlements offer a living example of this circular imagination,
which emphasizes the "ideal equality of households and family
units" and illustrates how "such circular arrangements can
form part of self-conscious egalitarian projects" (295). Sites like

Nebelivka and these Basque settlements prove that highly egalitarian organization is possible on an urban scale, thereby expanding the archive of collective freedom.

The last few decades of archaeological research, Graeber and Wengrow point out, have radically revised our understanding of the historical record of "premodern" societies. These examples suggest how civilization does not come as a set package of inseparable parts: large settlements do not require hierarchy, and so-called primitive democracy is far from crude or unsophisticated (297). Popular councils and citizen assemblies were forms of government not just in Mesopotamian societies. City-dwellers largely governed themselves: murder trials, divorces, and property disputes seemed to be mostly in the hands of town councils (301). As C.L.R. James said of fifth-century BCE Athens, "every cook can govern;" so, too, in ancient Mesopotamia, even being a manual laborer did not exclude one from direct participation (302).[24] According to Graeber and Wengrow, it is almost impossible to find a city in the ancient Near East without some equivalent of a popular assembly.

These societies not only developed sophisticated egalitarian institutions but created democratic forms of governance. Graeber and Wengrow locate the origins of social housing and democracy in ancient Teotihuacan. This was an urban community at a human scale (343). Few citizens were deprived of the basic goods of social life, and "many citizens enjoyed a standard of living that is rarely achieved across such a wide sector of urban society in any period of urban history, including our own" (343). Families lived in single-story buildings equipped with integral drainage facilities and finely plastered floors; each family had its own set of rooms with private porticoes. Even the more modest apartments evidenced a comfortable lifestyle, including access to imported goods and a "staple diet of corn tortillas, eggs, turkey and rabbit meat, and the milk-hued drink known as *pulque* (an alcoholic beverage fermented from the spiky agave plant)" (343). Authority was distributed through local assemblies, likely answerable to a governing council (344). This was not merely a blip in a historical trend of centralized authority, but instead an anticipation of what would develop as the Indigenous critique of settler colonial political forms soon to approach from the east.

The story of ancient Teotihuacan points to the crux of the problem for Graeber and Wengrow. Contemporary social scientists tell themselves that Europeans introduced democracy to the Americas, and that this came as a single cultural package: "advanced metallurgy, animal-powered vehicles, alphabetic writing systems and a certain penchant for freethinking that is seen as necessary for technological progress" (349). In this story, "Natives" existed in "some sort of alternative, quasi-mystical universe" where political constitutions or sober deliberation over collective decisions simply didn't take place. On this reading, democracy is a gift of Europe; it is a modern invention that comes with a set range of social practices delimiting the possibilities of human freedom.

With this story, Graeber and Wengrow write, we are dealing with "powerful modern myths," myths that they contest with the second basic move in their work: historicizing the Indigenous critique, which includes showing how Enlightenment ideals of freedom were indebted to Indigenous practices of freedom in the absence of state organization and social hierarchies (350). Graeber and Wengrow elaborate the Indigenous critique by showing how questions of social inequality originated in the encounter between settler colonists and Indigenous inhabitants of the Americas. Kandiaronk, strategist for the Wendat confederacy and a Huron-Wendat chief, exemplifies the critique that gave rise to these ideals. A remarkable orator, skillful politician, and staunch opponent of Christianity, Kandiaronk had a long history of negotiating with Europeans. He may well have visited France in 1691 (51). The French Baron de Lahontan, a one-time deputy to Montreal's provincial governor fluent in Wendat and Algonkian, wrote three bestselling books about his experiences in the Americas. His *Curious Dialogues with a Savage of Good Sense Who Has Traveled* (1703) was structured as a dialogue with a character based on Kandiaronk. Lahontan's books had an enormous impact on European sensibilities in the eighteenth century, exerting an explicit or covert influence on figures such as Montesquieu, Diderot, Voltaire, and Rousseau (58). But Lahontan's influence is really due to Kandiaronk's eloquent critique of the very society to which Lahontan's readers belonged.

Kandiaronk's criticisms focus on Christian morality, the use of law, the state of morality among Europeans, and, most important, the inequality, unfreedom, and uniformity that typified European and settler colonial societies. The Europeans saw "savages" as poor, miserable, and unfree while Kandiaronk insists that the Europeans are the ones to be pitied—"I find it hard to see how you could be much more miserable than you already are" (54). Europeans must be forced to do good and only refrain from evil because of fear of punishment. Laws and law-suits both follow from a society organized around private property and money. Kandiaronk thus reverses the judgments Europeans leveled at so-called uncivilized societies: who are the real "savages" here, anyway?

In contrast to European depravity and misery, Kandiaronk opposes the relative freedom of Indigenous American societies such as the Wendat. Freedom according to Kandiaronk consisted in not being subject to external authorities. Precolonial Americans were equal "insofar as they were equally able to obey or disobey orders as they saw fit," which was exemplified by the democratic governance of the Wendat and Five Nations of the Haudenosaunee (45). In contrast to the rigid moralism of European Christianity, Kandiaronk speaks for the liberty of individuals bound only by common responsibilities as well as the immanent morality of mutualistic social organization. Kandiaronk thus articulates a critique of legal institutions as opposed to flexible practices of self-government, a critique of hierarchy as opposed to equality, and a critique of European vices—such as mendacity and covetousness—as opposed to the qualities that ought to define humanity: wisdom, reason, and equity (56).

Once again, the lessons of Kandiaronk should not be seen as the timeless, ahistorical rantings of a "primitive" people but as a constellation of lessons hard-won from historical experience. For Graeber and Wengrow, these lessons derive from an encounter with and flight from hierarchical societies in precolonial America. Located on the banks of the Mississippi River in what is now Illinois, the mega-settlement of Cahokia offers an example of this learning. This "first state" in America began as a place of pilgrimage. Around 600 CE, Cahokia began to develop social hierarchies and by 1050 CE exploded in size to include a population of 10,000 or more inhabitants. These hierarchies became worse; the ruling elite expanded its power, leading to the dissolution of nearly all self-governing communities outside the city as the urban core centralized power and authority. Within a century of the initial urban expansion, signs of violence and social decay showed themselves. A giant, palisaded wall was built encircling only some parts of the society and not others; the new elite apparently immured themselves within. By 1150, a long and uneven process of war, destruction, and depopulation began. By 1400 CE, Cahokia was abandoned (469).

What happened in Cahokia did not stay in Cahokia. As Graeber and Wengrow put it, Cahokia "appears to have left extremely unpleasant memories" (468). The disasters resulting from elite rule inspired a political and social shift across the Americas. "Petty kingdoms and the very practice of building mounds and pyramids had almost entirely vanished from the American South and Midwest" by the early eighteenth century (471). As the shadow of these hierarchical societies receded, egalitarian institutions emerged from self-conscious social movements: communal councils with equal say and processes of consensus-finding characterized the Nations known in the colonial period as the "five civilized tribes" of the American Southeast: Cherokee, Chickasaw, Choctaw, Creek, and Seminole (472). The Osage practiced self-governance in refusal of the social elitism exemplified by Cahokia (476). As interpreted by Graeber and Wengrow, "the ideals expressed by thinkers like

Kandiaronk only really make sense as products of a specific political history" (482). This helps explain the democratic organizations not only of the Osage but also the Iroquois or Haudenosaunee Confederacy. This is the context from which Kandiaronk—and the Indigenous critique—emerged.

Moreover, the Indigenous critique lies closer to the reflexive understanding of freedom today than the settler colonial beliefs that saw freedom as animalistic license ("wicked liberty," according to the Jesuits). The subsequent political sensibilities remain with us today: personal freedom, equality of men and women, liberal sexual mores, and popular sovereignty—"or even, for that matter, theories of depth psychology" (40–41). Graeber and Wengrow conclude: "In this sense, at least, the Wendat won the argument" (492).[25]

Graeber and Wengrow's account extends and deepens the history, practice, and theory of radical democracy, but it leaves several questions open. First, without something akin to a theory of morphic fields, they cannot explain the continuity between Teotihuacan, Cahokia, and Kandiaronk. Graeber and Wengrow have a gap in their account, acknowledging that "it would be going a bit too far to suggest" that the views of those like Lahontan were "the ideology that overthrew Mississippian civilization" (482). We argue that their excavation does more work than they envisioned—revealing not only continuous strata of collective experience that can reshape our imagination of what is possible, but also providing evidence for a morphic field of democratic aspiration both in resistance to and beyond the reach of hierarchy and unfreedom. This democratic field proves far more varied in time and space than scholars have previously considered. It suggests a more robust history of democratic aspiration and inspiration. We find it helpful to see this in terms of what Rupert Sheldrake calls a morphic field, as a species inheritance available not only through direct transmission, or through continuity of traditions—as Graeber and Wengrow assert—but also through a process of attunement. Understanding the continuity of the desire for collective freedom across vast timespans and disparate spaces as a morphic field shows how an immaterial force has in*formed* and can continue to in*form* the actualization of democratic desire across diverse peoples and places.

Second, while Graeber and Wengrow usefully emphasize the freedom of human groups to form collective life as they wish, this focus on human agency does not sufficiently examine the ecological interdependence both limiting and facilitating the expression of human freedom. Perhaps due to their leeriness of environmental determinism, Graeber and Wengrow leave little room for ecological entanglements between human freedom and the more-than-human world. Graeber and Wengrow work with a determinism-freedom binary that has the effect of disappearing more-than-human actors. This binary obscures how human freedom is always earthly, which is to say entangled with (and interdependent with) systems and lifeforms outside the reach of full human control (and with agency of their own). Graeber and Wengrow fail to acknowledge this earthly, embodied dimension of earthly flourishing, betraying a lingering anthropocentrism. Absent this acknowledgement, their account of collective freedom is severed from the habitats that sustain earthly flourishing—and upon which any human freedom is ultimately dependent.

Graeber and Wengrow's inattention to ecological entanglements is made more surprising because of how many of their examples illustrate cosmologies marked by deeply intertwined human and more-than-human actors. The Indigenous critique speaks to and elaborates a politics of ecological entanglement in profound and potent ways, but Graeber and Wengrow pass over this in silence. Third, their focus on deep history also fails to connect explicitly with the present moment, except in abstract calls for reimagining political possibility. They thus never let the living Indigenous speak. Aside from Kandiaronk (who's ventriloquized by Lahontan), the preponderance of their evidence comes from archaeological investigations. Turning to several Indigenous thinkers and examples of Indigenous practice today, we show how the capacious archive of democratic practice offered by Graeber and Wengrow's inquiries is also an archive of earthly entanglement and thus more-than-human as well as human democratic striving.

EARTHBORN(E) DEMOCRACY
AND THE INDIGENOUS CRITIQUE

It is preposterous, of course, to claim that we can "make the Indigenous speak:" Indigenous people do not have a singular voice, nor would we want to claim we could make them speak in monotone. Graeber and Wengrow's use of the term

"Indigenous" implies something that we would not claim, because of its generality and abstraction from particular contexts of enunciation. Perhaps for this reason they appear cautious about ventriloquizing any particular community, staying at the abstract level of "deep history" where the only common features are general commitments to freedom. Be it out of caution or an overriding focus on human freedom, Graeber and Wengrow neglect certain features of extant Indigenous cosmologies and lifeways that do not fit their narrative, but which we see as essential for developing an account of earthborn(e) democracy. Our purpose here is not to romanticize Indigenous knowledges or cultures but, rather, to attend to how the brilliance of these practices illuminates the world we inhabit differently.

Listening to Indigenous communities underscores how many forms of extant Indigenous thought and praxis begin from the bedrock assumption of earthly entanglement, both of the terrestrial and the spiritual and ecological entanglement of the human and more than human.[26] Entanglement is not something to be escaped, as modern understandings of freedom would have it, but rather something to be embraced. Instead of a politics of disentanglement and, with it, unfettered freedom built on control of the more-than-human world, earthly entanglements provide the roots and connections that allow for genuine freedom to come into being. Attuning to earthly entanglements awakens a greater aliveness to the experience of freedom and the earthly flourishing in which it plays a part. Therefore any account of democratic freedom adequate not only to this moment of ecological crisis but also to the underlying facts of earthly living must begin from an awareness of terrestrial existence—our earthborn(e) life. Such an account also must include the possibility of attunement to seemingly immaterial or invisible elements of collective life: wishes, dreams, memories, stories, connections and obligations to ancestors and descendants, and an awareness of the entangled nature of past, present, and future. Drawing upon this thought and praxis, and putting them into conversation with a deep history of democratic aspirations, can displace, if not eventually replace, anthropocentric accounts of politics, culture, and history. The emphasis on both aspects of entanglement within Indigenous thought and praxis can encourage re-storying the modern myths named by Wolin as well as Graeber and Wengrow to better facilitate earthborn(e) democracy.

In *Braiding Sweetgrass*, Robin Wall Kimmerer, a member of the Potawatomi Nation, and trained biologist, argues that modern, scientific knowledge has only just begun to take seriously ideas of mutualistic ecological entanglement that were well known to Indigenous societies. Kimmerer's interest in Western science began with a question that appeared to be nonsensical from within that framework: why did goldenrod and asters look so beautiful together? Kimmerer persevered in her field even as her motivating questions were marginalized and regarded as neither objective nor disinterested. Kimmerer's subsequent writings argue that scientific knowledge must now catch up to Indigenous ways of knowing regarding how humans thrive within mutualistic relationships with the earth and its creatures, or else suffer in absence of such relations. She points to emerging evidence surrounding how our connection with the earth resembles in both power and form our connections to other human beings, pointing for example to studies that demonstrate how the smell of humus releases the same hormonal response that mother and child experience during breastfeeding.[27]

Kimmerer's vision of—and increasing evidence for—multispecies mutualism, helps to generate a politics of earthly entanglement that moves beyond Graeber and Wengrow's anthropocentric freedom. Kimmerer does so by emphasizing the history and knowledge of species interdependence, not just the normative claim but also the fact of mutuality. She underscores the sensual development and experience of these facts through close connection with land and its dynamic complexity, such that humans develop a greater awareness of where they live and what's happening there. The land is the one with the power, as Kimmerer demonstrates and reiterates throughout her work. For Kimmerer the earth's power exists only through concerted cooperation of the human and nonhuman. Power is generative, multispecies, and cocreated. "All flourishing is mutual," declares Kimmerer.[28]

The cultivation of sweetgrass provides a narrative arc for Kimmerer's account of earthly flourishing pursued through ecological restoration. For Kimmerer, sweetgrass is more than a useful plant and a source of medicine; it is a nexus of praxis, story, and the unbreakable link between the two. Interacting with the materiality of sweetgrass, according to Kimmerer, is a means of reconnecting to that which has been repressed. As Kimmerer writes:

Hold out your hands and let me lay upon them a sheaf of freshly picked sweetgrass, loose and flowing, like newly washed hair. Golden green and glossy above, the stems are banded with purple and white where they meet the ground. Hold the bundle up to your nose. Find the fragrance of honeyed vanilla over the scent of river water and black earth and you understand its scientific name: *Hierochloe odorata*, meaning the fragrant, holy grass. In our language it is called *wiingaashk*, the sweet-smelling hair of Mother Earth. Breathe it in and you start to remember things you didn't know you'd forgotten.[29]

Sweetgrass detoxifies landscapes and restores habitats, providing gifts for humans and nonhumans alike. Yet sweetgrass's flourishing also depends on human care and attention. "The earth endows us with great gifts," Kimmerer writes, "[but] the other half is that the gift is not enough . . . we participate in its transformation."[30] Like Walter Benjamin's involuntary memory, the act of smelling sweetgrass transports us to vital awareness of interspecies mutualism, directly accessed through sensuous experience that can be mediated and passed down through narratives and stories.[31]

The work and gratitude of human beings "distills" the sweetgrass. Sweetgrass thrives with human attention or languishes without it; so, too, the stories that Kimmerer tells (including the story of sweetgrass) require human attention and enactment: not just repetition but also iteration or adaptation that preserves the spirit of the encounter and the relationship.[32]

Across manifold beautiful and interwoven stories in *Braiding Sweetgrass*, Kimmerer elaborates how Indigenous traditions have developed rituals to pursue this mutual flourishing. The Honorable Harvest names one such "prescription for sustainability."[33] Honorable Harvest rituals vary across different cultures and ecosystems, but all locate human beings within distributed agencies involving multiple creatures, human and nonhuman alike.[34] While unwritten, the rules of Honorable Harvest are "reinforced in small acts of daily life:" respectful relationship to that which one must consume in order to live; awareness of and reluctance to exceed one's own needs; and gratitude and reciprocity in gift-giving relationships across time and space.[35] When the norms of the Honorable Harvest are violated, complex and dynamic systems are thrown out of balance, which results in suffering to all participants—even if that suffering remains largely unconscious. The stunted human imagination of the modern, settler colonial world (and its legitimating myths) refuses to extend agency and interest beyond the human, leaving most people unaware of the destructive consequences of their violations.

This same imagination of the modern, settler colonial world also denies the spiritual register of earthly life that is so present in Indigenous thought and praxis. For Kimmerer, once you acknowledge earthly entanglement you've already entered a spiritual realm. However, restoration of relationships between plants and peoples is often seen as separate from engagement with anything immaterial. Scientists "have learned a lot about how to put ecosystems back together," but their experiments focus on "matter, to the exclusion of spirit."[36] Dwelling only in the material world (and being bound solely to material needs) encourages the appearance of what the Anishnaabe people call the Windigo, a monstrous villain of tales told on freezing north-woods nights.[37] Windigo represents an exclusively material life, a dwelling apart from the immaterial aspects of life (fig-ured as relationships with ancestors, stories, and dreams).

For Kimmerer, indigeneity is a way of being in the world, not exclusively a social status. Although non-Indigenous peo-ples may face structural obstacles to becoming Indigenous, Kimmerer does hold out the possibility that settlers can become "naturalized to place." This requires the recognition "that your ancestors lie in this ground . . . to live as if your childrens' future matters, to take care of the land as if our lives and the lives of all our relatives depend on it. Because they do."[38] For Kimmerer, none of this makes sense outside of a cosmology that is both material and immaterial: relations among species as well as spiritual connections across time, culture, and language. With-out such a cosmology, we are left alone and lonely, bereft of all our relatives and the lessons for earthly flourishing they could provide.

Rootedness, then, for Kimmerer is not just rootedness in place but rootedness in a spiritual existence that transcends place, time, and species. This provides people with the capac-ity for resistance and renewal. As Kimmerer writes of the Indig-enous people who survived the cultural genocide perpetuated by Indian residential schools: "Despite Carlisle, despite exile, despite a siege four hundred years long, there is something, some heart of living stone, that will not surrender."[39] As she puts it elsewhere, "Generations of grief, generations of loss, but also strength—the people did not surrender. They had spirit on their side."[40] Grief lives on within an Indigenous critique, resonating beyond any single particular life; it represents a fractured link between "land and people, between the past and the present that aches like a broken bone still unknit."[41] But "grief can be comforted by creation, by rebuilding . . . fragments, like ash splits, can be rewoven into a new whole."[42]

Integrating these traditions and contemporary politics, Kimmerer updates political concepts such as consent and nation and reframes these through earthly, reciprocal relationships. The rules of the Honorable Harvest, Kimmerer writes, would lead to "the democracy of species."[43] Kimmerer's description of "Maple Nation" provides a way to envision such a democracy where the boundaries of membership exceed both human jurisdictions and the jurisdiction of the human. In Maple Nation, declaring citizenship goes beyond paying taxes; maples, for example, are recognized for their key work in sustaining ecological vitality: creating habitat for songbirds, building soil through falling leaves, purifying air and water, and storing carbon (to name a few of their civic contributions).[44] In such a political imaginary, ecological bioregions replace state boundaries. These ecological regions are defined by the leading denizens of the region: Salmon Nation in the Pacific Northwest, Pinyon Nation in the Southwest, and Maple Nation in the Northeast.[45] Each of these iconic beings does their part to facilitate balance in the ecosystem; taking up citizenship in these nations means asking ourselves, as humans, what we are doing for them.

Being a good citizen of Maple Nation, Kimmerer writes, requires sensual aliveness to scent, taste, and texture when learning how to take care of the trees. As one of Kimmerer's interlocutors, Mark, puts it, living our earthly citizenship involves reciprocal relations: "You make syrup. You enjoy it. You take what you're given and treat it right."[46] In her stories, Kimmerer emphasizes the ways in which sensuality can create connections and relationships across species boundaries. These restored relationships can then serve as a basis for social and civic learning and action. An acknowledgement of interdependence stands at the root of these relationships; this interdependence requires conceiving agency in distributed terms, such that each participant in a complex system requires others to act. Instead of imagining how to "include" species in existing political systems, then, Kimmerer prompts us to envision political systems on the basis of distributed agency. We are already embedded in networks of mutuality and distributed agency—we are always already being ecological, in Timothy Morton's words.[47]

Kimmerer prompts her readers to identify rituals that could embody the reciprocity inherent to ecological politics. An ecological politics for Kimmerer re-envisions political concepts like nation, citizenship, and law on the basis of ecological entanglement. For instance, "Maple Nation" defines a terrestrial-political zone that is more real than the lines and divisions of existing political geography, because it reflects the central intuition that the land is the one with the power.[48] The norms of the Honorable Harvest articulate rituals of reciprocity within such polities. Together, Maple Nation and the Honorable Harvest illustrate how addressing earthborn(e) democracy requires rethinking existing political jurisdictions, standing, and citizenship, shifting all of these toward what Kimmerer calls "the structure and function of the natural world that make life possible."[49]

Kimmerer's writing bears beautiful witness to human and nonhuman entanglement, but she does not elaborate the democratic politics of this entanglement. Graeber and Wengrow give us a more capacious political history of collective freedom while Kimmerer orients life toward entanglement; here we want to show how these are mutually intertwined. Democratic flourishing depends on (and in turn nurtures and sustains) ecologically entangled habitats; earthly flourishing consists in the mutual supportive relations between practice and habitat, activity and resonance field. Any account of democracy without attention to its need for an ecological holding environment to enable the development of democratic capacities remains incomplete.

The language of morphic fields and resonance suture together Graeber and Wengrow, on the one hand, and Kimmerer, on the other, by theorizing the holding environments for democratic life. For Graeber and Wengrow, the practices embodying the three essential freedoms are learned traits in response to specific historical situations as well as collective needs and desires; though they overlook the potential reach of their account, the theory of morphic resonance gives language for seeing how these practices might spread without direct transmission or be available for renewal despite periods of discontinuity.

The practices and rituals Kimmerer describes, by light of the theory of morphic fields, constitute these fields while being in*formed* by the existent fields themselves. The habitats and the practices are thus two sides of the same coin.

As mentioned above, the shrinking of democratic aspiration in modernity is an *environmental* problem. It's not simply that the environmental space ("nature") is what democracy ("culture") needs. One is impossible without the other. The nature/culture distinction resembles the material/immaterial distinction within the theory of morphic resonance; morphic resonance, however, illustrates how material practices are in*formed* by immaterial fields and the immaterial fields are the *deposits* of species experience. These deposits have resonance that lies beyond sensory perception; they are immaterial but begin as material. Just as caterpillars spin silk to create an environment in which they can transform, humans improvise on the basis of capacities for negotiation, care, and creativity; the resonance of these experiences in turn constellate as fields to in*form* and in*spire* future improvisations (actions, practices, etc.). Democratic practices are an environmental phenomenon—just like the caterpillar's silk—and the range of available or normative practices is a question of ecology as much as atmospheric gasses or the water cycle.

There remains a question of how to mediate between the development and reiteration of intentional capacities for collective self-governance and the informing fields of resonance. Kimmerer's descriptions and performances of attention-giving in her writing hint at a possible way of sounding out the echoes between past and present, but what is missing is an account of attunement across specific traditions or peoples that can suggest how democratic chreodes can be re-created. In the section below, we describe this work of mediation in terms of *attunement*.

ATTUNING TO RESONANT HISTORIES: THE EXAMPLE OF TREATY PRAXIS

Some two centuries ago, a Ktunaxa hunting party was tracking a herd of deer over northern Rocky Mountain passes. To hunt deer for the Ktunaxa meant more than just the provision of meat; it also involved them in reciprocal, cross-species relationships expressed through the ritual of their Blacktail Deer Dance. On this occasion, the deer brought the Ktunaxa into the hunting grounds of the Piikani. Soon enough, the Ktunaxa encountered a Piikani hunting party, sparking a conflict with potentially dangerous consequences. Immediately, a council was called to negotiate the situation. According to the story, the Ktunaxa acknowledged their transgression, but spoke of how their actions were required by the mutual, sacred obligations to the deer. To right their transgression, they offered the Piikani the rights to the powerful medicine ceremony of the Blacktail Deer Dance. This created a reciprocal sharing between peoples whose impact continues today.

Brian Noble, who recounts this version of the story, notes how ongoing political dynamics between the Piikani and Ktunaxa continue to resonate with its lessons. For Noble the story illuminates what he calls "treaty praxis" and its attendant ecologies.[50] This describes the interface between the spiritual, ecological entanglement, and social freedom.[51] To quote Noble: "This was a praxis of treaty, animated by an ecology of sharing in the land and its fruits, of exchange, reciprocity, mutual obligation, extended relations through ceremonial-material encounter among persons, animal-persons, animal collectives, and peoples' collectives—a cooperation of Ktunaxa, Piikani, and blacktail deer."[52]

The resonance pattern of treaty praxis has been obscured by colonial epistemologies,[53] just as Graeber and Wengrow's account of collective freedom has been obscured by the dogmas of modern anthropology, archaeology, and political science. Coloniality constrains, hardens boundaries, and creates separation; it veils the morphic field of the species and the entanglement and interdependency among different species fields. Treaty praxis, on the other hand, "keep[s] people, animals, worlds, and the complex among them all at play, responsively and symmetrically."[54] Participants maintain their rootedness in place while fashioning new relations with other rooted beings, finding commonality in their shared activities. Ecological entanglement thus involves a dance of play and rootedness: one must be rooted in a sense of place and its obligations and responsibilities (limits); yet at the same time this sense of rootedness opens the possibility of play with others that might take the form of acknowledging other similarly rooted forms of life. The Piikani and Ktunaxa could negotiate reconciliation by recognizing each other's rootedness and the interplay among these roots. Building on Graeber and Wengrow, it is not the ability to walk away that enables human freedom but rather a capacity to root in place that enables nego-tiation of a free existence. What appears to be a paradox in Graeber and Wengrow (as well as most accounts of modern freedom) is one of the key starting points for earthborn(e) democracy.

Treaty praxis attends to how multiple species are involved in reconciliation of potential conflicts. In the example of the Blacktail Deer Ceremony, a respect for and responsibilities to the gift of the deer prompted both the Piikani and the Ktunaxa to find common ground together and peaceably share the fruits of the hunt. Treaty praxis emphasizes how rootedness in place can form the basis for reaching moments of commonality across differences rather than being a license for exclusion or some-thing that homogenizes particularity.

Entanglement is not just a material phenomenon or practice; as Kimmerer reminds us, it involves making kin with the ances-tors and spirits of a place.[55] The theory of morphic resonance maintains a nonsectarian (scientific) openness to these not merely material entanglements. The theory also (like Kim-merer) calls attention to that which many materialist accounts, such as Graeber and Wengrow's, cannot countenance. For instance, another version of the Blacktail Deer Dance empha-sizes how earthly flourishing necessitates an attunement between the material and immaterial.

> Long ago in their camp one of them died. The one that died was a man true and good. After he died, his spirit went away to the land of the dead to find out what was there. When he had been there a while, the spirit told him to return to his

people and tell them what was there. He had been dead seven days, and his body was badly decomposed; but the spirit of the dead took his spirit down to its body and he came to life. He came to life in the midst of his friends. Now it was this way: the watchers around the body heard a noise inside of the corpse, but all the while the spirit of the dead man was sitting near, saying that he was trying to sing. So they quickly unwrapped the body. Then the man opened his eyes, and, looking at them, said, "I have come from the land of the dead. I have come to teach you more songs and prayers." Then he rose and picked up a small bell. Now all the people were very hungry, for they had nothing to eat for a long time. The man said, "Now we will dance." So he led the dancers round in a circle, and, keeping time with the bell, sang the songs he had learned when in the land of the dead. When the dance was over, the people rested while he prayed for them. Then they danced again. They all slept that night, and when they awoke, the man who had been dead said, "I know all about power. I saw it in my dream. You can believe that there is such a place." Then the men went out to hunt and brought home a great deal of meat, and after that the dance was called the "Black-Tail Deer-Dance." Now everyone takes part in this dance before he goes out to hunt. They dance in the evening, and at night they can see in dreams where game is to be found.[56]

This version of the story offers a rich illustration of many of the themes of this chapter. First, it shows how morphic fields, stories, and rituals are intertwined, with each dependent on the other. The morphic field of multispecies adaptive mutualism interweaves with the story of the dream, which then prompts the dance as a ritual connected to a broader myth of what we would call earthborn(e) democracy. The story is a means of attunement to resonance fields. Rituals manifest the learning that can come from attunement, providing means of embodying the lessons that emerge from the dreamwork. "Now we will dance," calls the man, who then rings the bell and leads the dancers in a circle. Once the dance is over, the man prays: the Black Tail Deer Dance is an emergent ritual embodying broader myths of reciprocal entanglement and distributed agency ("I know all about power"). Fields persist through the work of attunement, and stories are the primary mechanism of attunement for the human species. Attunement involves both attention to the vibrant matter that surrounds and imbues us and the immateriality of the fields or habitats of possibility. Stories like the Following Deer story hold both these senses: they call for deep attention to themselves—their words, their rhythms, their surfaces—while also instructing listeners and readers to attend the world to which they point, a world filled with resonance, where the past is present and where spiritual and material realities are simultaneously present.

Attunement to resonance fields allows for regeneration and renewal. Attunement is the means by which species actualize latent forms, even when material (generational, genetic) links have been broken. Attunement initiates and continues the process of re-storying and restoration. The "ache" of a broken bone, "still unknit," as Kimmerer puts it, calls us toward adaptations that keep alive the resilient spirit to pursue what we call earthly flourishing. Graeber and Wengrow's three modes of freedom—to move, to disobey, or to transform—also name adaptations that ultimately protect and preserve democratic aspirations, as does fugitive democracy for Wolin (even if he understates its historical breadth and depth). The future of earthborn(e) democracy depends on attunement to the morphic resonances we have described in this chapter. "Newness is renewal," perpetual and unending.[57]

THE MORPHIC RESONANCE
OF EARTHBORN(E) DEMOCRACY

This chapter advances a rereading of the "recurrent aspirations" for democracy through a theory of morphic resonance. This helps us to constellate and recontextualize emerging archaeological evidence of "prehistorical" democratic self-governance along with Indigenous thought and practice, both historical and enduring, to see continuity and commonality across disparate times, places, and cultures. The stories reread in this light suggest how earthborn(e) democracy could resonate across these examples, in*forming* contemporary strivings for democratic life *as* earthly flourishing.

The theory of morphic resonance offers a way of understanding the persistence and process of democratic aspirations. There is a memory in nature, including within the human species, that exceeds written records and oral traditions, but is held within a field encompassing, surrounding, and informing the behavior of the species. The memory of past democratic moments thus informs the present. A theory of morphic resonance, for example, connects the otherwise discrete historical experiences of Cahokia and the Indigenous critique of Kandiaronk. The experience of self-governance and collective freedom (as well as the species experience of domination exemplified by Cahokia) influences the field in ways that appear in collective memory, both conscious and unconscious, of the species. The reappearance of these forms across space and time is more than coincidence or mere contingency; it is the presence of the past.

Although the mythless myth of modernity continues to propagate and enlarge anti-democratic resonance fields, Cahokia (among other examples) reminds us that anti-democratic patterns have persisted across history and are not particular to the contemporary moment. Within a habitat where examples like Cahokia resonate so strongly, the development of democratic capacities faces long odds. The crisis of democracy is, in essence, a matter of habitat loss. These facts suggest the need for new myths as a means of attunement to, and reinforcement of, these democratic aspirations, which have a deeper continuity and broader reach than previously imagined. Democratic flourishing will require a kind of rewilding—a rewilding of democratic capacities, which would in turn initiate a rewilding of the democratic habitat.[58]

For the great scholar of myth Mircea Eliade, myth takes us to the *illo tempore*, the dawn of everything, when all was first conceived of and created. Being connected to the dawn of everything is the means by which humans connect with the origins of their practices and self-understandings; myths are the source of renewal if those practices or self-understandings become hollow or are lost. Myths provide orientation towards the reasons for existence and the possibility for understanding and embodying the purpose within those reasons. The iterative process of renewal represents the way the species carries forward, corrects, and develops the organizing structures of their collective existence. For Eliade, though, the new is always tied to the archetypal patterns stored in the collective unconscious.

Graeber and Wengrow borrow the title of their monumental work from Eliade, yet within their text there is an ambivalence towards myth that is left unresolved. On the one hand, they write that "we all live in myths: just as all societies have their science, all societies have their myths. Myth is the way in which human societies give structure and meaning to experience . . . but larger mythic structures of history . . . [over] the past several centuries simply don't work any more" (525). These myths include a progressive account of history, and a corresponding rejection of the archaic as primitive and vice versa. For Graeber and Wengrow, their counter-historical archive is intended to overturn the unspoken myths of modern archaeology and political science, but they do not consciously offer an alternative. As a result, they risk carrying forward an aspect of the modern mythology of anthropocentric self-fashioning. Their emphasis on what they call the third basic freedom of collective transformation betrays an implicit Promethean politics that sits uneasily with the cosmologies of Indigenous lifeways that constrains the agency of humans in light of interspecies entanglement. Graeber and Wengrow's idea that we can draw upon counter-histories primarily to "reshape our conceptions of who we are and what we might yet become" is modernist at its core.

In the terms of our argument, democratic life requires myths in order to flourish. Earthborn(e) democracy seeks to re-story democracy and attune practices of self-governance to fields of possibility while emphasizing the necessary entanglements between democratic and earthly flourishing. Myths for democratic flourishing can attune us to our earthborn(e) natures, helping us to recognize conscious and unconscious desires for collaborative, multispecies mutualism. Myths are stories that reconnect us to the sheer possibility of origins while also grounding us in the archetypal pathways by which the life of species has unfolded. Myths are not just stories of what it would mean to live in right relationship with the world; they are also a means of inquiry into that world and how to best respond to emergent problems of the moment. Democratic mythmaking involves mediation between science and spirit, material and immaterial, story and ritual. Myth and science always go hand in hand, but in the last two hundred years their relationship has been repressed and made unconscious because of unexamined and anthropocentric myths of human omnipotence. Modern (unspoken) myths obscure the work of attunement to the earthly entanglements that a myth of earthborn(e) democracy makes central. The deep histories of Graeber and Wengrow, the Indigenous cosmologies and epistemologies attending the Honorable Harvest and the work of treaty praxis, and Wolin's emphasis on the recurrent aspiration for democracy constellate together within this myth. While Graeber and Wengrow understand their counter-histories as "roads not taken," they remain available—and increasingly necessary—pathways for democratic forms of life (524).

We need a myth of the earthborn(e). First, however, we need to inquire more into how myth works. In the next chapter we turn to depth psychology to explore and to populate the myth of earthborn(e) democracy, by tracing archetypal resonance patterns of democratic freedom and flourishing—freedom born through earthly entanglement rather than achieved in separation from it. The resonant histories recounted in this chapter invite, if not require, a corresponding account of depth psychology to realize the creative potentials of earthborn(e) democracy to become unstuck from the twinned crises of the present moment.

Chapter Two

THE EARTHBORN(E) UNCONSCIOUS
AND DEMOCRATIC ARCHETYPES

*Without history there can be no psychology, and certainly
no psychology of the unconscious.*
—Carl Jung, *Memories, Dreams, Reflections*

We need to rise from history to mystery.
—Norman O. Brown, *Love's Body*

THIS CHAPTER moves from material counter-histories, indebted
to emerging archaeological studies as well as historical and
extant Indigenous traditions, to immaterial psychic realities that
imbue earthborn(e) democracy. David Graeber and David Wengrow write to fire the imagination of future alternative worlds;
we contend here that such work requires an inquiry into depth
psychology to reveal an earthborn(e) concept of the unconscious.
This earthborn(e) unconscious represents a collective history of
earthborn creatures, the psychic analogue of the geological
record studied by geo-scientists. Just as climate scientists ana-
lyze ice-core samples pulled from glaciers, here we envision
probing the psychic depths accumulated across earthly history,
which have been repressed by modern myths of human self-
making. The earthborn(e) unconscious appears as dreams,
fantasies, symbols, images, and ideas that recur and resurface
across space, time, and culture. This record is both collective

and individual, both human and nonhuman, both articulable and elusive.

While it may seem as though the age of myth has receded and, hence, that the concept of a collective unconscious is archaic and passé, we argue that dreams, fantasies, and symbols still orient collective life today despite the modern fetish of rationality. The technological fantasies of geoengineering and space colonization—to name but a few—are old stories in new containers, the latest iteration of what Max Horkheimer and Theodor Adorno named the myth of Enlightenment.[1] Here we argue, in the context of the climate crisis and the sixth mass extinction, the site of political struggle is as much poetic as it is practical. As Adrian Parr asserts, "Imagination is one of the biggest challenges environmental politics faces."[2] Not only are we locked into structural patterns of consumption and production that threaten the biosphere, but we are also stuck in a collective story that reinforces these patterns. For Parr, this story consists of an "apocalyptic imagination," which treats climate change as a source of spectacle and titillation rather than a public concern necessitating sustained political will and action. This imagination rests upon tropes of heroic masculinity and messianic salvation, which only serve to feed, and do nothing to overcome, the dread and anguish associated with ecological catastrophes. Instead, for Parr, we need "emancipatory imagining . . . adept at aligning difference and solidarity."[3] While Parr focuses on a relational account of imagination that pairs an outward orientation toward difference with an inward-looking critical reflection, in this chapter we argue that an ecological politics of the imagination must embrace the inescapable influence of myth. Perhaps the best tool for illuminating the resilient power and importance of myth is the tradition of depth psychology.

Our turn to depth psychology is informed by recent arguments for bringing psychoanalysis into contemporary political thinking. As Amy Allen has argued, psychoanalysis offers a "realistic conception of the person" that can both temper naive optimism about human perfectibility while also providing a theoretical foundation for social transformation.[4] For Allen, psychoanalysis grounds critique neither in utopianism nor rationalism, but within a realistic yet hopeful account of the human psyche that countenances the aggression and destructiveness to which the species is susceptible while also emphasizing capacities for creativity, reparation, and care. In making this argument, Allen draws upon Joel Whitebook, who maintains that psychoanalysis avoids "joyless reformism" only by maintaining a "robust notion of the unconscious," which nourishes sociopolitical imagination.[5]

Such a notion of the unconscious also calls for an appreciation of the necessary relationship between imagination and the resonant power of myth. Here our account is informed by the work of Carl Jung, who famously asserted the inherent relationship between myths and the unconscious. Myths are the attempts of fallible humans to trace and encompass the complexities of life that are, ultimately, beyond comprehension. Myths are to the social as dreams are to the individual: both are psychic phenomena, but myths have a broader and deeper psychosocial significance. So-called disenchanted modernity is anything but; the rationalism of modernity is itself an unacknowledged myth—the myth of Promethean self-making to overcome the chthonic forces of the earth *and* the psyche. The myths of modernity, however, leave modern subjects psychically bereft and democratically impoverished, by estranging humans from earthly entanglement.

Here we draw upon Jung to offer a robust notion of the unconscious that can fill out the dreams of collective refashioning to which Graeber and Wengrow, Allen, and Whitebook point while also attuning this work of reimagination to the roots of earthly entanglement that modernity has disavowed. We cannot simply begin anew and leave history behind, but neither can we see history as prologue; rather, we must, in the language of Norman O. Brown, rise "from history to mystery," to dreams, myths, and visions and the power they limn. To pursue this inquiry, we begin from Jung's theories of the collective unconscious and archetypes. Breaking from the overly personalized psychology of Sigmund Freud and many of his followers, Jung proposed the collective unconscious as the living psychological inheritance of the species. The collective unconscious cannot be fully known or mapped, according to Jung; its contents, however, pass through to consciousness in what he calls archetypes.[6] Archetypes are forms representing possibilities of perception and action within the life of the species.[7] Although Jung's theory has often been read in a conservative, if not reactionary, vein—in part because the archetypes seem to imply a rigid determinism—we argue that the collective unconscious and its archetypes allow us to understand the "recurrent aspiration" for democracy identified in chapter 1. The archetypes can reveal roots of, and nourish imagination for, democratic flourishing in moments of crisis such as the present one.

While Jung's concepts of the collective unconscious and the archetypes offer potent tools for building a notion of earthborn(e) democracy, Jung himself did not sufficiently elaborate the political implications of his insights. Thinkers as diverse as William Ophuls, Noëlle McAfee, and Félix Guattari have, in different ways, taken up the challenge of considering the relationship between politics and the unconscious. Ophuls emphasizes the lawlessness of the unconscious and the need for ethical and political constraints in line with the truths of ecology; McAfee calls for a politics of working through the traumatic, ongoing residues of history lodged in the unconscious; and Guattari views the unconscious as a reservoir of creative energy for political projects yet to be undertaken. All these thinkers, however, miss the opportunity to consider how the archetypes include democratic forms, something that Jung also overlooked. We take this up in arguing for democratic archetypes of flight, sociality, and politicality.

The democratic archetypes, importantly, are also earthborn(e). Jung on occasion glimpsed the earthly nature of the unconscious but did little to develop this idea. Yet everything within the psyche is of the earth. We articulate the earthborn(e) unconscious by emphasizing the seemingly paradoxical relationship between earthly rootedness and creative natality: we are *borne* by the earth and *born* from it as emergent beings. Geo-philosopher and cultural ecologist David Abram makes explicit the relationship between the unconscious and the earth,

THE UNCONSCIOUS AND DEMOCRATIC ARCHETYPES

helping us to develop a myth of the earthborn(e). Attuning to what Abram calls "the commonwealth of breath" leads us to comprehend fractious interdependence with one another, human as well as nonhuman. Each of us breathes on our own, yet our breathing brings us into relationships with the whole of the earth. Finding forms for developing these relationships toward mutual flourishing is the work of earthborn(e) democracy.

THE COLLECTIVE UNCONSCIOUS
AND ARCHETYPES

Jung's theory of the collective unconscious implies a deep history of the psyche that parallels Graeber and Wengrow's deep history of the species. Composed through patterns of behavior and action accruing over the life of humanity, the collective unconscious traces a record analogous to the archaeological record Graeber and Wengrow have studied, with both holding deposits of accumulated collective life that hold alternatives to the present order of things. Unlike Graeber and Wengrow's deep history, however, which requires extensive excavation and analysis to understand, the collective unconscious is never far from the surface of daily human activity, even if it remains resistant. Glimpses of its forms come through dreams, stories, myths, and symbols. "The man of the past is alive in us today."[8]

Jung distinguished between personal consciousness, the personal unconscious, and the collective unconscious. While the personal unconscious contains contents that have been repressed

or forgotten by the individual psyche, the collective unconscious, "as the ancestral heritage of possibilities of representation" is not individual but common to all human beings—
"perhaps even animals"—and is the "true basis of the individual
psyche."[9] Here Jung saw himself as faithful to Freud, who
viewed the unconscious as the "true psychic reality," which was
"collective . . . [and] a general possession of all mankind."[10]
However, Freud, unlike Jung, shied away from emphasizing the
collective nature of the unconscious in the interest of developing a scientific theory for individual mental disturbances. Jung,
on the other hand, explored the collective unconscious through
comparative mythology, which allowed him to study what he
considered "a sort of projection of the collective unconscious."[11]

The collective unconscious is not a personal acquisition, and
it exists independent of personal experience.[12] Consciousness is
shaped through personal experience, but consciousness is always
held within the deeper structures of the collective unconscious.
The collective unconscious thus acts as a "timeless and universal psyche" continuous across space and time; it "contains the
whole spiritual heritage of mankind's evolution, born anew in
the brain structure of every individual."[13] Raising the collective
unconscious to consciousness can have a therapeutic effect, by
collectivizing what was previously felt as merely individual, recognizing that seemingly idiosyncratic desires and dreams are
held within the collective unconscious. By tapping into this "living picture" that contains "pretty well everything that moves
upon the checkerboard of the world . . . a sense of solidarity
with the world is gradually built up."[14] Seeing our individual stories within a broader tapestry can arouse feelings of love and

sympathy across the typically narrow boundaries of affection and identification.[15]

Jung considers the collective unconscious to be an empirical matter. It is necessary for explaining the appearance of enduring patterns of behavior across cultural contexts—and their correlates in dreams, stories, and myths. However, because the collective unconscious always remains in the background of human awareness, it is difficult to diagnose its impact on our personal and social lives. The archetypes form the bridge between the unconscious and consciousness for Jung. The archetypes are preexistent forms and categories regulating the instinctual forces of the psyche. The instincts, for Jung, are typical modes of action, that is, regular expressions of energy in response to recurring situations, which become nearly automatic depending on the regularity of repetition. The instincts and the archetypes together form the collective unconscious. The instincts are the river; the archetypes are the riverbanks. Jung writes, "From the living fountain of instinct flows everything that is creative."[16] The archetypes contain and channel—*inform*—this creative flow.

Engraved on our psyches through repetition, archetypes are as numerous as typical situations. Everyday roles, with "immediate realities" such as "husband, wife, father, mother, child" form the most well-known archetypes; "eternally repeated," Jung says, these "create the mightiest archetypes of all."[17] Jung gives the example of the Holy Trinity, which consists of Father, Son, and Holy Ghost. Here we have the archetypal family, which repeats itself in the Catholic formulations of Christ as the bridegroom, the Church as the bride, and the baptismal font as the womb of the Church.[18] The archetype is the enduring form into which the particular images are incorporated, which means that particularities can change even if the broader pattern remains stable.

Jung admits that the archetypes themselves contain more than any given instantiation or interpretation (such as the baptismal font) can convey. They turn something "horribly alive" into a "beautiful abstraction."[19] The beautiful abstraction is the only way the overwhelming power of the archetypes—which "are so packed with meaning"—can be encapsulated and embodied.[20] Archetypes are excessive, and they have blurry boundaries. Not only does the river shift course ever so slightly with each season, but because of that the riverbanks—the archetypes—must also be seen as living, dynamic, and irreducible to any moment of their realization.

While the archetypes themselves are "hypothetical and irrepresentable," they function as "universal images that have existed since the remotest times," with a kind of weak transcendent power dependent upon repetition of experiences.[21] The archetypes form an invisible system of reactions and aptitudes that guide the life of the species behind the scenes. Archetypes are "systems of readiness for action," which exert a powerful psychic influence.[22] In other words, the archetypes are not an inert depository or garbage dump. The ghostly life of the archetypes demands the blood and sweat of the living, extracted through rituals of enactment. Rituals enflesh archetypes through iterated and attuned collective practice.

Myths and fairytales, for Jung, represent the primary ways that human cultures interact with and narrativize these psychic patterns, which precede and encompass those communities. Myths thus hold archetypal resonance to which ritualistic patterns of behavior attune. For Jung, the reappearance of archetypes in narratives across time and space provides evidence of their "elementary" or "primordial" nature.[23] While the archetypes structure and canalize the pathways of human imagination and practice, their dependence on repetition also opens the possibility of their alteration or reconstruction over (deep) time.[24]

Jung's theory of the archetypes has come under criticism in (at least) two ways. First, Jung's example of the Holy Trinity illustrates how he appears to affirm the patriarchal family structure and elevates European myths to archetypal status. Second, Jung's romanticization of so-called primitive Indigenous cultures suggests a simplistic, chauvinistic view of non-European peoples. These critiques are clearest in light of neo-Jungians such as Robert Bly, who take up warrior-archetypes in a non-developmental and ahistorical way.[25] Feminist responses to Jung, however, have emphasized how the archetypes are necessarily made and lived, not predetermined; they must be "brought 'down to earth,'" says Demaris Wehr.[26] "The images feel sovereign, but they aren't unchangeable," adds Susan Rowland.[27] The archetypes themselves may appear conservative, but Jung consistently maintains that human creative powers arise in relationship to these forms, "like Nature herself—prodigiously conservative, and yet transcending her own historical conditions in her acts of creation."[28] Attunement to the depth psychology of the archetypes is, seemingly paradoxically, the very condition for the emergence of adaptive or creative improvisation.

Humans always must "dream the myth onward" into futures that are inherently open.[29] Their dreams are always born(e) within fields that precede, support, and hold them.

Putting Jung into conversation with Graeber and Wengrow allows us not only to explore the inexhaustible depths of the archetypes but also to radically expand archetypal situations to encompass the newly revealed deep histories of the species.[30] Graeber and Wengrow make available a previously unknown archive of experiences from which to educe hitherto neglected archetypes. Their emphasis on cooperation, mutualism, non-hierarchical forms of collective life, and playful and flexible patterns of settlement shifts stories from heroic individuals to resilient and innovative communities. In other words, the marriage of Jung and Graeber and Wengrow can generate new images, stories, and myths of politics capable of channeling creative energies toward democratic futures in light of the newly revealed—and more deeply democratic—past.

THE POLITICS OF THE COLLECTIVE
UNCONSCIOUS AND ARCHETYPES

Jung was not a sophisticated political thinker, but he warned that neglecting the collective unconscious could have disastrous effects in political life. "Archaic symbol[s]," Jung observed in 1936, can invoke "mass emotion" to influence and revolutionize the lives of individuals in a catastrophic manner, alluding to National Socialism in Germany.[31] The riverbanks will either direct flow in democratic or undemocratic directions, meaning that to neglect the politics of myth is self-defeating. Not treating the collective unconscious with appropriate care can only result in the return of the repressed.

While naming the potential dangers of manipulating the collective unconscious and the archetypes, however, Jung did not develop the more constructive political possibilities of his theories. Three contemporary political thinkers—William Ophuls, Noëlle McAfee, and Félix Guattari—trace possible political pathways emerging from a grappling with the collective unconscious. Each path can flesh out aspects of the recurrent aspiration for democracy, limning what we will call democratic archetypes—forms of democratic striving—available for the ongoing projects of earthborn(e) democracy.

For Ophuls, the value of Jung's work lies in its orientation toward the "primordial drives and conflicting emotions" that humans "only partly understand and struggle to control."[32] Humans have paleolithic psychology in the midst of industrial civilization with its godlike technologies; this civilization is a thin, superficial development resting on a deep, animalistic foundation. For Ophuls, the inner life of the species is volatile, hostile, and conflicted. The rationalist vision of human perfectibility is—because of the transhistorical power of the instincts and the collective unconscious—impossible and ultimately undesirable.[33] It is impossible because humanity's ability to plumb the depths of the instincts and unconscious will always fall short; it is undesirable because the unconscious is also the source of our deepest desires and longings, which will never be satisfied by rational solutions but will press to find outlets in myths, dreams, and visions that adumbrate its mysteries without trying to reduce or resolve the unconscious completely.

While Ophuls's diagnosis may exaggerate the violence and cruelty of humanity, his prescription is highly Jungian. In response to this "cautionary portrait" he calls for a tripartite collective response of therapy (*therapeia*), education (*paideia*), and politics (*politeia*).[34] Therapy can restore unity to the psyche by reconnecting us with the disavowed unconscious, both personal and collective. Education is therapy "writ large"; it can not only restore unity but also elevate the psyche toward achievable levels of excellence.[35] Politics provides the means for inculcating social norms and mores—statecraft as soulcraft. "True liberation," Ophuls concludes, "comes from within": educational and political institutions must be reformed to reflect this.[36]

Politics, for Ophuls, is ultimately about the definition of reality.[37] Politics must go farther than mere institutionalization—it must foster new mythologies: "a nobler new fiction that offers the means of long-term survival and the prospect of a further advance in civilization."[38] The nobler new fiction is based on the Gaia hypothesis—that the earth is more like a living cell rather than an inert rock. According to Ophuls, only an eco-myth (to replace our modern myths) can allow human beings to make sense of their world and the suffering to which finite life is subject. Such a myth requires poetry that "foster[s] cognitive and intellectual sanity" and gives "powerful, beautiful, and authentic stories of who . . . humans are and what we should do with our lives."[39] Politics necessarily requires a civic religion that "provides personal orientation, moral guidance, and a framework for public order without imposing dogmas that must be believed or priests who must be obeyed."[40]

Ophuls's argument ends up in a reconstructed republicanism, reminiscent of Jefferson's and Tocqueville's visions of small-scale democracy, while bridging Jung's depth psychology and developments in quantum physics and the science of ecology. For Ophuls, this vision is the most realistic blueprint for harmonious social life and harmonious living with nature for a deeply unharmonious species. McAfee, by contrast, acknowledges the insights of depth psychology to offer a therapeutic model of liberal-democratic politics that emphasizes a collective capacity for acknowledging and working through historical traumas and their enduring effects. Unlike Ophuls's philosophical anthropology, which skews toward the unshakable archaic "man" within us all, McAfee's psychodynamic model of politics draws upon feminist philosophers and psychoanalysts who view human development as the evolution from speechlessness to participation.[41] An inclusive public sphere thus provides the basis for human development, as it allows for the translation of frustrated desire into communicative action.

McAfee centers the political project of democratically engaging collective conflicts in a way that distinguishes her from Ophuls's project of managing the basis of these conflicts through educational institutions. Yet there are different levels of conflict: the everyday disagreements that compose a democratic polity versus the deeper sources of stasis residing in the collective unconscious. The collective unconscious, for McAfee, is the primary site of the unresolved effects of historical trauma. She maintains that "democratic work . . . can help release bodies politic from the grip of past traumas and ongoing fantasies of foundational origins."[42] Democratic work comprises six key practices: imagining politics as public practice; having a self-understanding as citizens, not subjects; identifying and thematizing public problems; deliberating with others; harnessing public will; and radical questioning. Together these constitute "the wetlands of democracy" where McAfee centers the "contingent, fraught, and easily derailed" passage to "reflexive sociality."[43] If taken seriously, these six practices can animate public life, providing citizens with a sense of agency and mature connection to one another. Even if there is a somewhat tragic acceptance of the inevitability of loss and trauma, McAfee offers a therapeutic democratic politics in which the repressed memories of historical violence can be identified, named, and worked through.

For both Ophuls and McAfee, the unconscious is a depository for deeper patterns that organize public life and residual traumas hidden from public view. The unconscious is an inheritance from an archaic past that has not passed. By contrast, for Guattari, the unconscious is not a testament to which we are bound; rather, it is something to be built. According to Guattari, "to work the unconscious . . . is not simply to discover it, but to lead it, to produce its own lines of singularity, its own cartography, in fact, its own existence."[44] For Guattari, accepting the collective unconscious requires transforming psychoanalytic practice into collective activity, which he terms "schizoanalysis." "The first positive task of schizoanalysis is discovering your desiring machines . . . independent of any interpretations."[45] This discovery of desire enables lines of flight. "Desire finds itself trapped" by archetypal models, but desiring-machines "live on the order of dispersion."[46] Guattari writes, "psychoanalysis ought to be a song of life, or else be worth nothing at all. It ought, practically, to teach us to sing life."[47] Unfortunately, psychoanalysis attempts to limit or constrain the discovery of desire; it sickens or weakens the sources of creative flow—"sick desire stretches out on the couch."[48] For Guattari, the unconscious is a laboratory, not a depository, or as Franco "Bifo" Berardi puts it, it is "not a theatre but a factory."[49]

For Guattari, there is no single recipe for organizing institutional practices around the unconscious. Whereas Jung views the rhizome as rooted and arboreal, Guattari's rhizome is anarchic and processual. "It is a matter of constituting networks and rhizomes," Guattari says in an interview, "to escape the systems of modelization in which we are entangled and which are in the process of completely polluting us, head and heart."[50] We must escape the archetypes themselves—or so it would seem. "It seems to me essential," Guattari writes, "to organize new micropolitical and microsocial practices, new solidarities, a new gentleness, together with new aesthetic and new analytic practices regarding the formation of the unconscious."[51] Guattari refrains from prescribing any specific form for these practices and solidarities; he insists they must be experimental and open-ended.

Each of these three thinkers demonstrates an inherent relationship between the collective unconscious and the rituals that embody or instantiate myth. Ophuls's new "eco-myth" lives through the attunement with nature achieved by therapy and education. This myth forms the basis for a new sociality for political community, an ecological civic republicanism. McAfee's liberal-democratic myth envisions key practices of attuning to residual effects and affects of historical trauma—working through collective losses—in order to realize democratic capacities necessary for shared governance. McAfee envisions a politics of working across differences in light of the historical and enduring traumas residing in the collective unconscious. Guattari's processual and radically open account of the unconscious betrays a myth of perpetual self-creation, which requires practices of reformation and flight toward the new. The politics of the collective unconscious in all three theorists emerge through these formative, collective rituals.

As compelling as these three readings of politics and the collective unconscious are, a more capacious and generous conception of the collective unconscious and the archetypes is necessary to show the depths of democratic desire and possibility. To do this, we bring all three of these perspectives together to begin a reconceptualization of the archetypes in a more democratic direction. Politics *is* poetry—a struggle over the ruling metaphors and myths that ensure ecological survival. The collective unconscious is *both* laboratory and depository, a reservoir of conflict and cooperation but also of longing and desire for new forms of life. Democratic practices of working through are necessary but not sufficient, requiring imaginative lines of flight and innovative rituals as much as deliberation and accountability. Each of these articulations limns a specific archetypal pattern—of creative lines of emergence, harmony amid ecological entanglement, and cooperation across difference—that compose part of what we refer to as the democratic unconscious, which is earthborn(e).

DEMOCRATIZING THE ARCHETYPES

Archetypes are the imprints of the collective unconscious on psychosocial life. They themselves are not directly accessible, but they spark perception and imagination by resonating between present-day experience and the memory of the species.[52] For Jung, archetypes are the residue left by the repetition of typical situations in human life recurring throughout the deep history of the species. As our interpretation of Graeber and Wengrow illustrates, experiments in democratic organization have appeared more frequently across the sweep of human history than previously understood or assumed. The study of the archetypes, however, has not caught up to this new understanding of history, instead being largely focused on nondemocratic forms of social organization—on the family and church, and on individual heroes and authority figures—as resolutions to collective problems. Here we explore archetypes within the hitherto-neglected record of democratic experimentation— democratic archetypes that have persisted across space and time despite being overlooked by twentieth century scholars of depth psychology, not to mention nearly every democratic theorist since Jean-Jacques Rousseau. We organize our discussion around three key democratic archetypes: flight, sociality, and politicality.

FLIGHT

Recall the story of Cahokia, the pilgrimage site that grew to a large settlement in what is now Missouri, which over time centralized power in the hands of a ruling elite. In Graeber and Wengrow's account, this settlement appeared to co-opt and colonize self-governing communities outside its boundaries and it became increasingly hierarchical, leading to a proliferation of social maladies including constant surveillance and awesome spectacles of violence. As we know all too well from the historical record, this situation is recurrent—namely, elite domination over and against popular self-governance.[53] But just as this pattern recurs over time, so, too, has resistance in the form of flight: exit from domination or flight toward freedom, if only in the imagination.[54] In the case of Cahokia, literal flight followed its rise—a long process of war, destruction, and depopulation in which people first spread out to the hinterlands and then ultimately abandoned the area altogether.

Flight animates all three of what Graeber and Wendrow see as the recurrent patterns of freedom: the freedom to move, the freedom to disobey, and the freedom to create or transform social relationships.[55] For instance, the 800-year gap between the discovery of settled agricultural techniques and their wide scale adoption gives evidence of a commitment to freedom of movement: freedom from the drudgery of year-round farming, freedom from raiding parties who would target storehouses, and freedom from tax authorities and centralized political elites. The freedom to disobey reflects the refusal of inequality, or of patterns of hierarchical authority that persist through compulsion.[56] The freedom to transform relationships is also a kind of flight, relying upon the imagination of new possibilities. For the Wendat, it was embodied by social practices and rituals surrounding dreamwork, referred to as *ondinnonk*, a "secret desire of the soul manifested by a dream."[57] Dreams, for the Wendat, were the language for "other desires" unmet by present realities, which remained "inborn and concealed" unless they were brought out through collective rituals of "dream guessing."[58] This parallels the experience of the Black Tail Deer Dance described in chapter 1 (it also shows how depth psychology long pre-existed Freud and Jung).

These three patterns of freedom limn what we call the democratic archetype of flight, elaborated below. Importantly, these freedoms exist in a shadowed relationship to three forms of domination according to Graeber and Wengrow: control over violence, control over information, and charismatic power. Domination attempts to control life through coercion and the restriction—by violence or other means—of pathways of exit.[59] Hierarchies of power restrict the flow of information to contain and to keep things (and people) in bounds, or boundaries.[60] Charismatic power has its own hold on the psyches of a people, limiting their imagination and capacities for resistance or emergence. Flight sees beyond these borders and imagines or instantiates new lifeways.

Guattari's theorization of the political unconscious provides helpful elaborations of flight as a recurrent democratic repertoire. To "work the unconscious," for Guattari, means leading it "to produce its own lines of singularity . . . its own existence."[61]

Reassembling a "de-alienated, de-serialized subject," Guattari argues, involves embracing a "processual" mode of becoming that produces its own existence, "engender[ing] itself as *existential territory*."[62] Deterritorialization—fleeing from the modelization of life imposed by institutional authority and the hegemonic world system—serves desire as "a process of singularization, a point of proliferation and of possible creation at the heart of a constituted system."[63]

La Borde, an anti-psychiatric clinic, founded by Jean Oury and where Guattari worked for almost two decades, offers a concrete example of imaginative flight from extant institutional realities. At La Borde, the walls and gates of the hospital were demolished; uniforms were eliminated; the roles of patient and doctor were occasionally reversed; and workshops, clubs, and other activities were set up, designed to offer patients different social experiences.[64] La Borde was, for Guattari, a laboratory in which therapy could break from hierarchical models and from the rigid training he undertook with Jacques Lacan. The practices at La Borde refused the idea of an unconscious that was static, eternal, or authoritative, as opposed to a fluid medium inviting and requiring experimentation. The point was not to identify the right technique for therapy but to escape existing institutional and imaginative confines to explore, create, invent and improvise. La Borde provided a refuge from the clinical psychiatric version of Cahokia.

Robin Wall Kimmerer's idea of Maple Nation, described in chapter 1, offers another example of imaginative flight. "Maple Nation" envisions reorganizing the life of the community around a bioregion's anchor species: Maple trees in the northeast

United States; Pinyon trees in the Southwest; Salmon in the Pacific Northwest. This vision refuses the present institutional arrangements such as state boundaries and corresponding membership criteria as well as extant (and anthropocentric) civic responsibilities and duties. In such a vision, political authority would shift from human jurisdictions and hierarchies to ecological systems defined by the "leading denizens of the region."[65] Maple Nation is a flight from modern mythologies— which estrange human beings from nature—and leads to an embrace of earthly entanglement. In this way, flight involves not just deterritorialization but also return to a neglected, repressed way of being in the world.

These three examples, we argue, together illustrate a democratic *archetype* of flight. Flight consists of practices or pursuits of disobedience, reorganization, and reimagining. We use the term *archetype* because these practices recur across (deep) time and (distant) space, reflecting their persistence within the collective unconscious. This archetype is democratic because it withdraws resources and allegiance from concentrations of power and settled hierarchies, reinvesting this energy into more inclusive and egalitarian alternatives. Flight depends upon and develops the people's "capacity to do things."[66] People can leave present circumstances, as in response to Cahokia. The people can flee institutional constraints and hierarchies to invent an alternative, as Guattari and others did at La Borde. The people can also reimagine and reorganize these circumstances, to create new possibilities from within the shell of the old, as does Kimmerer's Maple Nation.[67]

SOCIALITY

For sociality as a second democratic archetype, recall further Kandiaronk and the Wendat people from which he hailed. In the background of what Graeber and Wengrow term the "Indigenous critique," Kandiaronk offers a vision of egalitarian, autonomous societies.[68] The Wendat were concerned with substantive rather than formal freedom, which required relationships of mutualism and cooperation: "Mutual aid . . . was seen as the necessary condition for individual autonomy." In these societies, according to Kandiaronk (via Lahonton), there was little need for systems of punishment and law to enforce order: members instead pursued wisdom, reason, and equity as integral to self-government, seeing themselves as bound by reciprocal relationships more than self-interest. Individuals had autonomy while still living in an egalitarian society; personal freedom was not opposed to mutualism but conditioned by it. This arrangement, for Graeber and Wengrow, was a lesson from the experience at Cahokia—another experiment in freedom born of the catastrophes of centralized authority and the arts of domination.

Ophuls's appeal to virtue, and his antipathy toward societies organized by law, illustrates a contemporary example of sociality as an archetype. For Ophuls, "true liberation," as we noted above, "comes from within," not from legalistic structures that attempt (and fail) to restrain self-interested individuals bound only by a transactional social contract.[69] Uneducated appetite leads to overconsumption and ecological catastrophe. "If nature could be said to have an ethos," Ophuls writes, "it is mutualism—harmonious cooperation for the greater good of the whole that simultaneously serves the needs of the parts."[70] Ophuls's vision of the political world imitates this natural order where each member plays its part to maintain the health of the body politic. Ecology must become the primary metaphor for social and political life, such that mutualism and autonomy can coexist. Evolution is always co-evolution; competition and predation are facts of life but need not predominate. Following the ethos of ecology allows political communities to become "conscious midwives of Gaia" and to construct a "*politeia* that is sane, humane, and ecological."[71] The mutualism of Ophuls's eco-politics reflects sociality's emphasis on mutual aid, interdependence, and collective belonging in the context of earthly entanglement.

"We must conceive of politics in the light of ecology," writes Ophuls; this resonates with Kimmerer's emphasis on norms that reflect reciprocal economies of giving and receiving taught by the land.[72] Kimmerer's essay "The Gift of Strawberries" dreams of a gift economy shared by humans and nonhumans alike that further exemplifies the archetype of sociality, where gratitude and reciprocity are the primary currencies. Gift economies reorganize and transform perspectives on entanglements within the *oikos*: they change the orientations of givers and receivers from consumption to restraint and from self-interest to mutuality. For Kimmerer this sociality is a metaphor—we would call it an archetype—and though it cannot by itself undo the structures of the market economy encircling the gift economy, the former is itself a story—albeit one that has "spread like wildfire."[73] But, as Kimmerer notes, "It is just a story we have told ourselves and we are free to tell another, to reclaim the old one."[74]

The ritual of the Honorable Harvest also illustrates the archetype of sociality, through guidelines such as taking only what you need, using the land respectfully, sharing, giving thanks, never taking too much, and sustaining the ones who sustain you.[75] The "dishonorable harvest"—excess, waste, and unsustainable consumption—has become a way of life, but Kimmerer argues that the "canon" of the Honorable Harvest is "poised to make a comeback, as people remember that what's good for the land is also good for the people."[76] The "gathering mentality" of the Honorable Harvest can be "conjure[d]" by tapping into "wild ideas" of ecological entanglement and interdependent relationships with the more-than-human world.[77] In other words, Kimmerer speaks to the dreamwork of accessing and attuning to the collective unconscious, here represented by an archetype of sociality. Sociality for Kimmer, is not just about the society of humans, but about relationships across the species barrier.

Sociality as a democratic archetype describes forms of mutuality and transformative community recurrent across human history. Once again, archetypes exist as the residue of repeated typical situations of human communities—in this instance the situation of how to share resources and envision relationships and responsibilities within ecological systems. From within this archetype, people take themselves to be primarily eusocial and ecological beings, yet this communal orientation does not necessarily imply dull conformity or social compulsion, as Kandiaronk's descriptions of the Wendat illustrate. Mutual aid educates self-interest, because autonomy is the fruit of cooperation not its antithesis. The ruling metaphor of Gaia that Ophuls offers illustrates another dimension of this archetype: a vision or organizing framework that reveals relations of interdependence among humans and nonhumans, revealing the shortsightedness and destructiveness of the dishonorable harvest. Kimmerer's vision of gift economies and her remembrance of the Honorable Harvest reflect a mythic structure that emphasizes the values of reciprocity, gratitude, and cooperation—integral elements of the democratic archetype of sociality.

POLITICALITY

The archetype of politicality names the capacity to negotiate differences and reach commonality in situations of conflict. This archetype appears in practices and institutions of self-governance like local assemblies; ward systems; architectures prioritizing intervisibility and the generation of public knowledge; open meetings; decentralized authority structures; as well as norms of deliberation, consensus building, and participation. At the level of the image, politicality appears as circles, orientations of mental and material space of people toward one another. At the level of myth, politicality surfaces in stories of how different people come to share a deeper commonality, by creating a shared conceptual framework of who they are. As our discussions of Graeber and Wengrow show, such forms of politicality appear repeatedly across the human record. Recall Nebelivka and its great concentric arrangements that supported centuries of self-governance without warfare or the rise of social elites, as well as bottom-up processes of social decision-making. Recall the Basques' built environment that reinforces egalitarian practices, which unlike Cahokia's palisades and inner, elite citadel, arrange themselves self-consciously around an open public space. Recall Teotihuacan's political authority of their local ward assemblies supported by egalitarian housing projects—urban community at a human scale. Recall Mesopotamia's "primitive democracy" of district councils and assemblies of elders alongside popular councils and citizen assemblies that formed stable structures of self-government not just in Mesopotamian cities but also in colonial offshoots.[78] Recall, also, the Wendat village councils, held "almost every day . . . on almost all matters," which improvised not only a capacity for public speaking but also for consensus-making.[79]

The democratic archetype of politicality appears in stark contrast to conventional forms of rule. The Indigenous critique articulated by Graeber and Wengrow draws this out: the horizontality of cooperative governance as opposed to the verticality of hierarchies; the equal participation of all members as opposed to participation restricted to elites; and circular forms that convene participants without implying differences of authority as opposed to the tiered and walled forms of states like Cahokia. Politicality is reflected in processes of clarifying, understanding, and working through differences via deliberative fora, civic discourse, and practices of relational power building that infuse formal institutional politics with the catalyzing energy of social movements and civil society organizations.

McAfee's key democratic practices also elaborate how politicality might function as a democratic archetype. For instance,

McAfee's second practice is for the people to understand themselves as citizens and not as subjects. This is an image of politicality, ideally reflecting and reinforcing concrete practices of
self-rule such as deliberative fora, open and reflexive public discourse, and mechanisms of accountability including a symbiotic relationship between social movements and formal political systems. McAfee's six key practices require public venues
from which conflicts can emerge and can be worked through
as citizens reach for commonality across their differences. They
can enable citizens to loosen the grip of historical traumas to
better practice collective self-determination.

Politicality is reflected in Hannah Arendt's famous image of
the table, as that which joins together while holding apart.[80]
The Following Deer story from the previous chapter also illustrates the archetype of politicality by showing how commonality can be reached across difference. The story is also an example of treaty praxis, as the search for cooperative relationships
in moments of disagreement or potential conflict. Treaty praxis
is an ongoing and reflexive form that projects a promise of cooperation into the future. To persist, it must be reflective and
continual, because the discovery and rediscovery of the political is, as Sheldon Wolin would put it, an endless task. Politicality in this example involves the Blacktail Deer as partners in
the treaty relationship, illustrating how this practice involves
nonhumans as well as humans. Moreover, politicality holds
different identities in relationship to one another without shear-
ing off or otherwise effacing the sharpness of these differences.
The parties to the Following Deer treaty praxis—the Ktunaxa,
Piikani, and Blacktail Deer, remain Ktunaxa, Piikani, and

Blacktail Deer, even if their self-understanding is altered by a new relational dynamic.

As a democratic archetype, politicality names norms, practices, and institutions that facilitate finding commonality among differences. Politicality holds these differences in relationship, offering a praxis of reconciliation that is ongoing and polyphonic. Difference is what is stable, while commonality must be cultivated. Coming to an understanding with one another marks the fulfillment of politicality, but this understanding is always provisional, subject to revision, and dependent on the continuing efforts of differently situated participants. As Graeber and Wengrow help to illustrate, moreover, politicality has institutional and material shapes in the structures of self-government such as circular architecture, localized assemblies, and deliberative spaces. Politicality also implies a shared mental image or conceptual framework, which gathers the people together as a people, while ideally—as in the Following Deer story—remaining somewhat porous to other groups through the recognition of shared earthly entanglements. The shadows of politicality include stasis, civil war, marginalization, and exclusion, which are similarly reflected in anti-democratic institutional forms and built environments, such as the exclusive enclaves for the rich protected by the walls at Cahokia.

WHY DEMOCRATIC ARCHETYPES?

Jung's theories of the collective unconscious and archetypes allow us to surface how the deep history of mutual aid, self-organization, and collective governance in the archaeological and written records has a corresponding psychic imprint. Because archetypes are timeless and universal, naming them makes them available to support and strengthen aspirations for democracy. Attunement to the democratic archetypes of flight, sociality, and politicality connects us in a new and vital way to the deep history of collective struggle for freedom.

The new materialist theory of assemblages offers a helpful contrast with our language of archetypes. Jane Bennett takes from Baruch Spinoza the idea that "bodies enhance their power *in* and *as a heterogeneous assemblage.*"[81] This means that agency is distributed across a field rather than being localized in a particular agent or humanly created collective. Recall Kimmerer's example of sweetgrass and the assemblage of actants involved in its flourishing: mineral, animal, and otherwise. Bennett's most concrete example of assemblage is the electrical power grid, which involves diverse elements that work together even though their coordination does not rise to the level of an organism."[82] The assemblage, while it includes human constructions, also involves nonhuman actants: "electrons, wind, fire, electro-magnetic fields."[83] The concept of assemblage provides a horizontal cross-species understanding of agency. The field of an assemblage is localizable in space and time, even if it is ultimately characterized by unpredictability. Assemblages are not agents, only "the effervescence of the agency of individuals acting alone or in concert with each other."[84]

Without rejecting the theory of assemblages, we see the theory of democratic archetypes as providing more expansive resources for envisioning democratic flourishing, for two reasons. First, a theory of archetypes provides more historical and psychological depth than a theory of assemblages, which is more presentist and emergentist. As we elaborate more in the next chapter, we understand emergence as a product of attunement to resonance fields or patterns of action and interaction that precede and encompass all life, even if they do not determine the expression of that life. Second, a theory of the archetypes opens access to the sheer fecundity of democratic experimentation within morphic fields—the repository that is also a laboratory. We agree with Bennett that agency cannot be limited to an individual, rational subject,[85] but the promise of democracy is the capacity to do things (*kratos*); the democratic archetypes hold the manifold history of this promise and can offer forms for creative democratic enactment.

The framework of archetypes highlights the depth psychodynamics of democracy. Individual psyches persist within a broader field of the collective unconscious, and archetypes are how the collective unconscious is translated into experience. The archetypes bridge the collective unconscious and individual consciousness in ways that can bring individuals into greater patterns of solidarity, both among contemporaries and within the history of the species. Democratic dramas and struggles, therefore, are never just about themselves; they are episodes within an ongoing and deep story spanning the history of human aspirations, energies, and freedom dreams. The memory of the living does not exhaust living memory. Archetypes are the residue of attempts to resolve typical situations and collective action problems. Graeber and Wengrow's monumental counter-history helps to fill in the record of these situations and shows how struggles for egalitarian existence across time are more common than the historical record has heretofore reflected, with its overriding emphasis on hierarchy, authority, and state-forms of power as the trajectory of progress by which humans move, inevitably, from "primitive" to "civilized."

Archetypes, by definition, persist over time and serve to organize and channel desire. But democratic struggles tap the excess of meaning that is also inherent to archetypes. Such struggles are inherently experimental and require creative improvisation—and they draw on the openness of the archetypes precisely to fuel such efforts, even as they reflect and reinforce deep patterns of action available to the species. Archetypes are not fully determinative but require the striving of the living to be enacted. As Jungian feminist Demaris Wehr emphasizes, archetypes are made and lived; they do not predetermine the expression of life.

Flight, sociality, and politicality, as archetypes, expand political imagination and open fields of practice for democratic life. Democratic theorists often pick up on one of these archetypes or another, but by expanding the view of democracy as a deeply historical and continuous field—containing many archetypes—we can comprehend broader and recurrent patterns previously unnoticed. Deliberative democrats, for example, often focus on achieving agreement across differences through practices of deliberation allowing for both mutual intelligibility and the retention of individual or group identity.[86] Agonist democrats or civic republicans, by contrast, tend to focus on cultivating political power in ways that exemplify the democratic archetype of sociality, which centers mutuality and cooperation—as well as contestation—among participants around common projects.[87] Embodiments of the democratic archetype of flight often avoid the language of democracy, couching their politics much more in the language of freedom as an escape from structures of domination and oppression to preserve or defend an imperiled or threatened identity.[88] We discuss ways that contemporary political movements tap into each of these archetypes in more detail in chapter 3.

It should be noted that these democratic archetypes are not exclusive from one another, and none exhausts the meaning of democratic struggle. Democratic theorists would do well to avoid elevating one archetype over any other, recognizing instead that the typical situations faced by freedom struggles are multiform, calling for a broad repertoire of possible responses. In other words, we should not emphasize politicality and its practices—of deliberation and consensus making, e.g.—at the expense of flight or sociality, which are also essential moments of democratic striving held within the collective unconscious. At its best, democracy would have all these elements in tense integration with one another.[89] Each of these archetypes reflects an aspect of the deeper truth of democracy as the development of the people's capacity to govern themselves free from domination.

Archetypal analysis reconnects democracy to constitutive myths, without becoming reactionary. Too often, democratic theory resists the lure of myths because of their supposedly archaic and conservative nature.[90] However, as Jung reminds us, we cannot live without myth. We are currently living within a modern myth whose mythic status is disavowed and hidden from view. Reconnecting to a theory of the collective unconscious and the archetypes allows democratic theorists to see the inevitability and importance of conscious mythmaking. As Ophuls and Kimmerer, each in their own unique way, remind us: the stories we tell about ourselves are the atmosphere that we all breathe.

Archetypal thinking may seem antithetical to emancipatory imagination. For Max Horkheimer, for example, there is no historical reservoir from which struggles for freedom can draw. "Critique," as he puts it, "has no custom on its side, even when it promises success."[91] Because archetypes draw on historical material, no emancipatory archetype would exist in Horkheimer's view. Yet as we have shown, a revised historical record teems with democratic experimentation. In this light, and as Norman O. Brown puts it, redemptive history is "anamnesis." We must "remember again what we have repressed," a "recollection of previous incarnations."[92] A democratic archetypal analysis gathers the repeated experiences of, and experiments with, flight, sociality, and politicality and shows their persistence within the surrounding, encompassing field of the collective unconscious. As Brown puts it, "the events sleep in their causes; the archetypal form is the hidden life of things: awaiting resurrection."[93]

To be clear, the democratic archetypes are not the only archetypes within the field. They exist in conflict with and are perpetually shadowed by anti-democratic patterns of action. Cahokia haunts the background of all democratic dreams. Flight is shadowed by containment and enslavement; sociality is shadowed by possessive individualism; and politicality is shadowed by stasis, division, and false consensus. The character Windigo, as narrated by Kimmerer and discussed in the previous chapter—the needy and insatiable "human being who has become a cannibal monster"—mythologizes this shadow.[94] Windigo is a human being grown monstrous through greed and fear. Windigo's avarice leads him to forget the web of reciprocity and to live a lonely existence in exile from human community.

The Windigo story needs continuous retelling because it illustrates the precarious pathways of collective flourishing. To tell the story of democracy one must tell the story of its shadows: Windigos are lessons and reminders of human frailty, which form part of the collective unconscious. Flight, sociality, and politicality never fully escape their shadows. "See the dark, recognize its power, but do not feed it," Kimmerer warns. Windigo embodies a fearful vision against which the freedom dreams of democracy must contend. Today's Windigos—instantiations of anti-democratic archetypes—continue to consume us to our and the earth's detriment.

A final reason for using the framework of archetypal democratic analysis is its potential significance for political movements. Compared with a theory of assemblages, people involved in political struggle can see themselves in this more expansive history: their activities and experiments are linked to the species' struggle for freedom. In a conversation with fellow activists, Grace Lee Boggs made this same point: "We want to illuminate the incredible, the unique grandeur of man."[95] The archetypes are a field to which we can attune, drawing from this field the inspiration, provocation, and strength for engaging in freedom struggles. And, yet, these struggles are always our own. They require our creativity, innovation, and the risk of starting something new. We must both attune to the power of myth and dream the myth onward.

THE EARTHBORN(E) UNCONSCIOUS

Although it may be easy to overlook, everything of the psyche is of the earth. We cannot understand the collective unconscious without understanding how it is a product of earthly entanglement. Earthly entanglement describes how all living beings on the earth are interdependent with one another. Consciousness, put simply, is made possible by the metabolism of breath, which in turn is made possible by reciprocal interactions of exchange with the world of plants. More than two-thirds of the human body is composed of water; the water cycle circulates through plants; animals (human and nonhuman); minerals; and atmospheric gasses. The calories burned through dreaming depend upon nutrients in the soil, deposited over centuries; and illumination and action depend upon energy sources drawn from millennia of organic decomposition.

While the above discussion of democratic archetypes has focused largely on human activities, the archetypes for Jung are products of the earth. In a suggestive yet undeveloped phrase, Jung claims that the archetypes are "the chthonic portion of the psyche."[96] By this he seems to mean not only that consciousness is built upon the earth but that the archetypes are the "most tangible" link between the psyche and the earth. He writes,

"The psyche is attached to nature," and the archetypes reveal "the psychic influence of the earth."[97] The collective unconscious, as constituted by archetypes and the instincts, is, thus, earthly and chthonic.

Still, while Jung's description of archetypes opens the door to thinking about the collective unconscious as an earthly reality, it falls short in several respects. For one, Jung maintains a sense of human culture's distinctiveness from nature, implying that culture requires growing *out* of the earth. Alongside this, Jung's depiction of the chthonic retains a chauvinistic view of other cultures and a patronizing gaze on the deep history of the species, as when he describes "reindeer hunters" who "fought for a bare and wretched existence against the elemental forces of wild nature."[98] Archaic forms of life are the "naked bedrock" of the collective unconscious upon which enlightened European civilization is built.[99] "Chthonic" for Jung thus comes close to "primitive" or "primordial" in meaning.

Unlike Jung's chthonic, by *earthborn(e)* we denote earthliness in two different ways: first, to be earthborn(e) is to be carried and supported by the earth—*borne* by the earth and dependent on its ecological cycles; yet second, to be earthborn(e) is also to be *born* out of the earth—to be natal, something new and miraculous, an emergent being not fully determined by the past. To be earthborn(e) holds a paradox: "everything new is old." To be *borne* of earth means to be constituted by earth; the flesh of the body is the flesh of the earth. We are composed of earth: "earth to earth, ashes to ashes, dust to dust."[100] Everything each of us *is*—every difference as well as every similarity—is of the earth: from it, in it, and bound to return to it. As David Abram puts it, "I realize the error of our common belief that we live on the earth. The rough-skinned rock beneath my feet is earth, yes, but what of those clouds, and the unseen sea in which those clouds are adrift? Are they not also part of earth? And if so, would it not be more true to say that we dwell *in* the earth, rather than on it?"[101]

As Abram suggests, humans are among the earthborne creatures. We are also *born* of the earth. Being born means we begin anew. This natality names the capacity for initiation, refreshed and revived through every new birth.[102] To be born *of* the earth is not always gentle; it is a rupture, a break, a new beginning that violates the old order. "Birth is bursting . . . the start is violent. The great heroic deed is to be born. . . . Every child, like Athena, is born fully armed; is a knife that opens the womb."[103] Initiation is individuation and differentiation—a separateness and distinction from other earthborn(e) kin.

Earthborn(e)dness, therefore, holds in tension the fact of our deep dependence on the earth as well as our recurrent capacity for (re)birth—that is, bringing new life to the earth. To be earthborn(e) is to be rooted, yet roots generate shoots—new directions, new tendrils. In one of Jung's most moving images, he describes how life is "like a plant that lives on its rhizome."[104] The rhizome is the continual source of life; what we see is the blossom, which passes. To be earthborn(e) is to be both rhizome and blossom. The rhizome contains the potential for everything, yet it is not everything.[105] The earth carries the seeds of new life. Life, as it emerges, brings something new into the world—a miracle.[106]

Earthborn(e)dness is the holding environment in which all archetypes, democratic and anti-democratic, contend. It is the *ur*-ground of all archetypal conflict; it forms the basis on which struggle, contestation, and disagreement take place—or, more precisely, it is the substance *in which* these conflicts take place. Archetypes are chthonic; they live within earthly material and thereby remind us of our earthly roots. Being earthborn(e) is a condition that cannot be dissolved or overcome, only forgotten or repressed—at great psychic and social cost.

Consciousness is earthborn(e), but modern human societies have obscured, disavowed, and repressed this fact. Modern myths of separation between human and nonhuman, mind and body, earth and spirit, have poisoned the self-understanding of modern subjects. These myths have codeveloped with structural shifts in modes of production, consumption, and debt that create vicious feedback loops intensifying their repressive tendencies.[107] We have disavowed the earthborn(e) unconscious; its apparent unavailability is an artifact of repression, the distressing symptoms of which are increasingly apparent.

As Jung says, it's not a question of living without myth; the question is what kind of myth do we live in. Mythlessness is rootlessness. At present, however, we maintain a myth *of* rootlessness. This is the story of modern Prometheus, of mastery and conquest over a nature external to human life. The fact that "myth" has come to mean something that is "untrue" or "primitive" is perhaps the cruelest twist of modernity's knife—which rests upon a myth so successful that its mythic nature goes unrecognized. By understanding modernity's myth *as myth* we can work to replace it with a better one. We need myths that heralds a way of living interdependently amid earthly cycles of death and rebirth: myths for earthborn(e) democracy.

A MYTH FOR EARTHBORN(E) DEMOCRACY

"What is the scale of breathing?" Alexis Pauline Gumbs asks:

> You put your hand on your individual chest as it rises and falters all day. But is that the scale of breathing? You share air and chemical exchange with everyone in the room, everyone you pass by today. Is the scale of breathing within one species? All animals participate in this exchange of release for continued life. But not without the plants. The plants in their inverse process, release what we need, take what we give without being asked. And the planet, wrapped in ocean breathing, breathing into sky. What is the scale of breathing? You are part of it now. You are not alone.[108]

The scale of breathing is the breadth of the earth. We live in what David Abram calls the "commonwealth of breath."[109] An earthly myth must contain the atmosphere as a medium of exchange and connection among bodies both human and non-human. As Abram also points out, the words for soul, mind, and spirit in most living languages have their roots in words for breath, respiration, or wind. Spirit is earthly, and the earth is spiritual. The earth includes the atmosphere, which is the earth's surface in which humans live. We live *in* the earth, not on it. This is why Abram spells earth as "eAIRth," to indicate the concentric circles of dependence between the individual "I," the broader biosphere, and the surrounding atmosphere.[110] Recall Kimmerer's description of sweetgrass, whose Latin name, *Hierochloe odorata*, means the fragrant, holy grass, and whose name in Kimmerer's language is *wiingaashk*, the sweet-smelling hair of Mother Earth. "Breathe it in and you start to remember things you didn't know you'd forgotten."[111]

Breath connects us, yet it also separates. As Luce Irigaray writes, "Our taking root corresponds to breathing by ourselves."[112] To come into life is to breathe on one's own. With our first breath, we define our space and place; it is our "first gesture" of coming into the world. Our breath accompanies us for the duration of our life, marking and defining this individuation. The Navajo term *nilch'i*, Abram writes, refers to both the "whole body of the air and the atmosphere" as well as "the air that swirls within us when we breathe."[113] The individual is not, however, a passive party with respect to this wind: "her own desire and intent (her own interior Wind) participates directly in the life of the indivisible Wind all around her."[114] The cultivation of interior wind allows individuals to influence and contribute to the exterior world. By cultivating well-being—*hozho*—of the interior wind, the Navajo can then "actively impart this state of well-being to the enveloping cosmos."[115]

Even though freedom comes from inhabitation within the commonwealth of breath, each new breath is a potential new path, a new way of moving in the earth. To be is to breathe, and all being is becoming. Breathing on our own allows us, as Irigaray puts it, to "leave prenatal passivity" and "simple contiguity with the natural universe."[116] Just as we regulate our breathing, we can shape our life. We can breathe in ways we haven't breathed before, which means we can act in ways we haven't acted before.[117] Breathing on one's own is the basis of freedom, another word for autonomy.[118]

Still, this freedom is always a return—a return to earth, eAIRth, the chthonic, Gaia. All democratic action takes place in the earth. For the earthborn(e), flight is not escape but return and renewal: movement away from one order and toward another still moves through the earth. "Newness is renewal."[119] Seen in this light, flight is restoration and regeneration. Sociality's pursuit of mutuality and cooperative autonomy also returns in a different way, tracing again to the relations of reciprocity and symbiosis that sustain ecological cycles. The differences that politicality assembles into commonality all consist of the same earth. To be earthborn(e) means understanding both sameness and difference as earthly. The commonwealth of breath unites us all in our differences, a fractious array.

The archetypes are reminders of chthonic roots, but they do not determine how we live out the condition of being earthborn(e). Attuning to the earthborn(e) unconscious can *inform* democratic practice, though the specific actions will vary from context to context. In other words, we resonate with the past but are not fully determined by it. We live on one earth, but the earth's topography is varied. You might find yourself in Cahokia, or you might find yourself in Teotihuacan. How to live out any given archetype, its specific relevance or resonance, depends on the circumstances. Our goal here has been to explore the depths, historical and psychological, atmospheric and terrestrial, of the repertoires and the range of tools with which to confront unfreedom—the full, abundant panoply of archetypal politics—in order to advance projects of earthborn(e) democracy. In the next chapter we turn to rituals of earthly entanglement to illustrate how earthborn(e) democracy requires the embodiment in rituals best seen in light of ongoing experiments for democratic life. Building out a myth of earthborn(e) democracy is not merely a question of the stories we tell ourselves but also of the actions undertaken in the world that exemplify the norms of reciprocity, mutualism, and emergence held within the archetypes.

Chapter Three

DEMOCRATIC RITUALS OF EARTHLY ENTANGLEMENT

Everywhere in these energized fields, resonance is drawing out new movements. Every root is a route, a flow, and thus every rooting is a routing, even at the most microbiological levels. And every movement has a frequency, and among the frequencies there are resonances. Every sinking into the dynamic specificity of place is also a microbiological exploration, extending and intertwining and inventing in countless ways.
—Romand Coles, Visionary Pragmatism

Can we imagine reconstructing our lives around a commoning of our relations with others, including animals, waters, plants, and mountains . . .? This is the horizon that the discourse and the politics of the commons opens for us today, not the promise of an impossible return to the past but the possibility of recovering the power of collectively deciding our fate on this earth. This is what I call re-enchanting the world.
—Silvia Federici, Re-Enchanting the World

One no and a thousand yeses.
—Zapatista saying

IN THE PREVIOUS CHAPTER we educed the democratic archetypes that form the broader collective unconscious. These archetypes are repeated patterns of coalescence, which hold possibilities for action in the present moment. Myth is the attempt to narrativize the persistent questions, problems, and possibilities of earthly life. Myth expresses itself through archetypes as well as plotting and relating enduring patterns, meanings, and places. Myth draws from the energy of the collective unconscious, and the condensation of this energy persists within archetypes.

Myth and archetypes, however, are impotent without rituals. Rituals enact and embody myth, bringing stories into being and materializing the archetypal forms in the present moment through iterated practices. Rituals are the means of participation in myth; they show how one lives out myth, makes it real, and makes it new, again. Our account of earthborn(e) democracy, then, is incomplete without an account of ritual. It is one thing to engage in conscious mythmaking about democracy in light of earthly entanglement; it is another thing entirely to show the ways in which myths are being lived out in disparate attempts to create more democratic forms of life. These experiments in democratic, earthly living are the subject matter of this chapter.

In the previous chapters, we argued that the myth of modernity has been built upon scientific rationalism, mind-body dualism, and the assumptions of Promethean mastery as the means of social progress. According to this modern myth, the age of myth is an archaic and regrettable part of human history, which can be glanced upon today with a condescending sense of superiority and relief. On this understanding, we have been freed from the constraints of myth. To be freed from the encompassing mythic background is to fully and finally claim the power to remake self, other, and world. Modern democracy, with its forms of the nation-state, constitutional system, and representational politics, has developed within this modern myth of self-making. In this respect democracy, in its current form, furthers the estrangement from earthly entanglements and the lessons of ecological interdependence.

In the modern myth, the demos seems to occupy the central place of power as the ultimate source of legitimacy and sovereignty. And yet the appearance of popular power is a masquerade that hides the people's powerlessness, which is the true content of this modern myth. The modern myth assumes political order requires the nation-state for stability and that the maintenance of this order calls for hierarchies of control and coercion.[1] Moreover, without access to the means of cultivating genuine political experience, the demos is habituated to periodic rituals and faux ceremonies of consultation.[2] The people must be represented because they cannot act; they must be managed because their direct participation threatens disorder. Agents of the state and multinational corporations are the primary actors while the demos is at best a passive spectator roused to occasional bouts of condemnation or assent, if their political agency is not actively suppressed entirely.[3]

By suppressing or repressing the power of the people, the modern myth has also bequeathed political rituals that lack authentic power. Rituals of modern democracy are largely restricted and reduced to participation within electoral politics.[4] The choice-making capacity of the demos is further sublimated into market-based consumerism, with political identity reduced to brand preference. In other words, modern myths tell a story of popular sovereignty that conceals a reality of popular powerlessness, in which substantive rituals of collective self-making are out of reach for all but a handful of elites, who themselves simply play according to rules not of their own making in what Joan Didion aptly called "Insider Baseball."[5]

In this situation, earthborn(e) democracy must not only contest myths of popular power/lessness; it must also offer rituals through which the people (*demos*) can create and express power (*kratos*). In this chapter we explore where and how people instantiate democratic power. We focus on rituals consonant with earthborn(e) democracy, and we position ongoing democratic experiments within an encompassing framework of ritual participation in myths of earthborn(e) democracy. Our examples seek to sensitize political actors and theorists to the potentials for creative action within contemporary democratic practice— potentials that emerge from attunement to fields of such action spanning space and time. Once again, our argument is that the twin crises of democracy and ecology described in the introduction that have arisen within modern myths have been aided and abetted by an impoverished repertoire of rituals for enacting popular power and attuning to ecological interdependence.

We foreground our examples of democratic practices of earthly entanglement with a discussion of theories of ritual. Rituals have long been understood as key practices for developing collective identity and belonging. They do this in part by drawing boundaries between the sacred and the profane while distinguishing mundane, chronological time from a time of significant transformation or metamorphosis, that is, kairotic time. While contemporary critics have lamented the "disappearance of rituals," we point to their persistence and potential role in further democratizing political life.[6] There is no democracy without ritual, we claim; it is rather a question of which democracy and what rituals. Our aim in this chapter is to investigate examples that enflesh myths of earthborn(e) democracy to attune readers to how the politics of ritual positions participants toward both attunement and emergence, preservation and possibility, continuity and innovation.

Our three chosen examples illustrate how democratic archetypes of flight, sociality, and politicality—articulated in chapter 2—are all embodied through political rituals. Glen Coulthard and Leanne Betasamosake Simpson's account of refusal of the modern settler state is rooted in ritualistic practices of grounded normativity—"ethical frameworks provided by . . . Indigenous place-based practices and associated forms of knowledge."[7] Cooperation Jackson, a radical experiment in democratic self-governance and eco-socialism in Jackson, Mississippi, with deep connections to traditions of Black nationalism and the history of Black cooperatives, illustrates rituals of emergence through participatory people's assemblies, cooperative development, and solidaristic economies that take into consideration both the human and more-than-human. Finally, the broad-based organizing politics in the contemporary United States exemplifies the interplay of rituals between attunement and emergence, how attention to lived experience, tradition, climate, and geography inform (without fully determining) political innovation and creativity.

Earthborn(e) democracy offers a vision that holds together these examples, which might otherwise appear disparate or dissonant. We aim to show a sheer multiplicity of practices of democratic experimentation slowly revealing the contours of possibility emerging from the shadow of modern myths of mastery and control. These examples of ritual enflesh myths of earthborn(e) democracy and show the way in which these myths might inform collective desires for democratic power. These place-based accounts offer both roots and routes, re-enactments of the species inheritance of collective freedom as well as new pathways for democratic aspiration. Rooting/routing is a process of reconstructing and re-enchanting life in terms of earthly entanglement, a "commoning," as Federici puts it, that includes "animals, waters, plants, and mountains." Democratic rituals of renewal blossom in multiform ways, a "thousand yeses" for the possibilities of emergent life and freedom. Earthborn(e) democracy is the rhizome from which these affirmations bloom—the perpetual, enduring field underneath the eternal flux.

DEMOCRATIZING (AND ECOLOGIZING) RITUAL

What is ritual and how does it relate to earthborn(e) democracy? According to Émile Durkheim, rituals are the means by which people tend to public things, sacred objects, and ideals. Rituals name and reinforce the boundaries of collective life, coalescing participants through shared experience. Within ritualistic practice, people gain a sense of themselves and their connections to others as well as their shared commitments. According to Robert Bellah's reading of Durkheim, rituals have three important dimensions. First, they require a group of at least two people in physical proximity to one another. Second, the members of this group must focus their attention on the same object or action, with the shared awareness of this collective focus. And third, these members come to share, through participation in the ritual, a common mood or emotion, what Durkheim calls "collective effervescence."[8] Rituals, according to Durkheim, "both express and reinforce collective representations and solidaristic emotions."[9] By attuning or paying attention to the same object or action, participants come to a shared, if implicit, agreement. As Robin Wall Kimmerer puts it, "attention becomes intention."[10]

Following Durkheim, Mircea Eliade argues that rituals distinguish the sacred from the profane. For Eliade, rituals are communal gateways that connect participants to transcendent realities. Similarly for Joseph Campbell, rituals invite the sacred, the more than here and now, into the present moment. Rituals mark off profane, linear time, inviting the possibility of transformative events. As Eliade writes, rituals are means by which participants "tap into primordial time and harness the forces of creation into re-creation."[11] Rituals then are practices of attunement to others, both proximate and beyond the here and now.

While attunement might sound inherently preservative or conservative—a process of maintaining continuity with the past—the experience of collective effervescence can also be seen as a means of radical, social improvisation. For Campbell, ritualistic participation in myth is not about the replication of authority but the regeneration of aspiration, which is the "motivator, builder, and transformer of civilization." Rituals organize the "energies of aspiration" and serve as the vehicle by which they are "evoked and gathered toward a focus."[12] Attunement forms the basis for emergence; ritual enactment never simply repeats the past without difference, but brings the past into being in a new way. In this respect, rituals are a process of freely drawing and redrawing the boundaries that encircle the community. Freedom, somewhat paradoxically, requires an encompassing horizon.[13] The enacted or performed character of rituals means that they have an inherent openness that allows for creative remembrance and adaptation.

The language of ritual, however, may seem to sound an archaic note. According to Byung-Chul Han, the age of ritual has disappeared. He argues the symbolic practices of ritual that allowed solidaristic communication have disintegrated in the face of compulsive demands to produce and consume under capitalism, which destabilize any enduring or inhabitable form of life.[14] Rituals once brought forth a community in which resonance occurred, creating a common rhythm and accord among community members. The disappearance of ritual is a crisis of resonance, a problem of attunement. "Without resonance we are thrown back onto ourselves, isolated."[15] Once rituals, in this traditional sense, have disappeared, modern subjects are "released" and "freed" from the protective horizons of cultural meaning, but these horizons are the holding environment in which individual and collective freedoms are born(e). As Campbell puts it, "the pathless way is the only way now before us," but the supposed freedom of this pathless way, opened through the disappearance of rituals, is a Pyrrhic victory, since the very conditions of freedom have been disavowed.[16]

Yet this account of ritual's disappearance overlooks the persistence of ritual in both religious and nonreligious communities. As Molly Farneth has argued, rituals of mourning in particular continue to appear in American public life, from funerals for those who died of AIDS organized by ACT-UP to Kaddishes for Black Americans killed by the police. Mourning rites offer symbolic practices available to believers and nonbelievers, marking events as transformative and interrupting chronological linear time. These rituals are the basis of re-forming communities and rearticulating collective values. Thus, Farneth argues, these rituals both reinforce solidarity and expand the boundaries of solidaristic concern.

For Farneth, the democratic potential of ritual lies in its ability to thematize, articulate, and correct for arbitrary exclusions as well as to accelerate a process of redistribution of goods such as social recognition. Yet more than creating more democratic organizations for the participants themselves, rituals, according to Farneth, can prefigure social and political alternatives, "enact[ing] structures and practices that anticipate the society" the participants hope for.[17] Farneth thus draws a line of thick connection between prefigurative politics and rituals: rituals are the means of investing action with symbolic or expressive intention, and they "anticipate a world that does not yet exist . . . nudg[ing] what currently is closer to what is not yet."[18]

Farneth provides strong evidence of the persistence of rituals as well as their democratic possibilities; here we complement her emphasis on the forward-looking, transformative nature of ritual with our concept of attunement as an equally important dimension. On our reading, the power of ritual derives from its process of attuning to the collective unconscious, the reservoir of longings, aspirations, dreams, and wishes that rest latent in the waking life of earthly beings. To borrow from Han, the resonance that ritual brings forth in community resounds in this vast, unexplored territory. Moreover, Farneth's account of ritual can be further extended to consider how ritual always takes place within a more-than-human world and contains implicit or explicit messages about the relationships between humans and the more-than-human. Attuning to the collective unconscious as well as the more-than-human world positions us to draw on the vast historical archive and emergent potential for earthborn(e) democracy.

Our understanding of ritual foregrounds the seemingly paradoxical relationship between attunement and emergence. This has special significance when considering ritual in terms of the earthborn(e). Attunement denotes how all earthly beings are *borne* by the earth: held and supported by it and dependent on it for continuing life. Emergence denotes how these same beings are *born* of and from the earth: how the earth is the condition of a natality that is never simply identical to the earth and its contents. Ritual thus marries the old and new, the conservative and improvisatory. Earthborn(e) ritual holds both senses in its "radical" (*radix*, from the root) nature: it roots participants by attuning them to one another, the past, and resonance fields of the species; it also routes participants—sending out roots that are routes, as Coles would put it—into new expressions, forms of subjectivity, and ecologically entangled assemblages of power.

Recall chapter 1 where we introduced the relevance of Rupert Sheldrake's theory of morphic resonance and morphic fields to our account of earthborn(e) democracy. Morphic resonance explains the continuity sustained through ritual performance and re-enactment. In this respect, morphic resonance retains the insights of Durkheimian structuralism and functionalism, or the durability of societal patterns across time. Yet it also allows for the ultimate indeterminacy of structure, which operates more like statistical regularity than determinative forces.[19] Fields in-*form* actions but do not fully determine them. The discourse of ritual calls attention to structural features of reality— the rhizome from which every blossom blooms. Attunement is the work of resonating with this structure and drawing from its power—the accreted energy stored up through patterns of repetition and reiteration. Rituals always take place within a morphic field of experience that is created and re-created through action across time and space. This field is populated by the archetypes, the virtual images and transpersonal psychic dispositions that are prior to individual experience.[20]

While Sheldrake insists that the theory of morphic resonance cannot explain change or transformation, we argue that attunement to morphic fields makes emergence possible. Participants tune into the species' capacity for creativity and agency. As David Graeber and David Wengrow note, certain rituals play a festival role for participants, keeping the old spark of political consciousness alive. "They allowed people to imagine that other arrangements are feasible, even for society as a whole, since it was always possible to fantasize about carnival bursting its seams and becoming the new reality."[21] As they put it, "Rituals are simultaneously moments where social structure is manifested and moments of 'anti-structure,' in which new social forms can pop up."[22] For Graeber and Wengrow, this description pertains to festive rituals that turn the world upside down, but this possibility of emergence inheres in rituals more generally. Because all rituals depend on the participants' intentional action as a group, ritual practice always relies upon and regathers the basic collective power that people acting in concert create—the power to create or re-create society (the *kratos* of the *demos*).

On Carl Jung's account, archetypes denote forms that represent and delimit possibilities of perception and action within the life of the species. As we argue in chapter 2, however, Jung overlooks what we call the democratic archetypes of flight, sociality, and politicality, which mark out the human and more than human capacities for re-imagining and re-creating social and political life. In other words, the democratic archetypes are deep structures and patterns *of* emergence, and it is by attuning to this historical archive and species inheritance that new actions or forms of life can appear in the world. Attunement to these forms opens the plastic possibilities for creative enactment. Ritual holds attunement and emergence together and thus avoids the apparent tension between a deterministic reading of the archetypes (i.e. *archē* as rule) and radical contingency and chaotic nature of free action (*an-archē* or refusal of rule).

How does this theory of rituals help to elaborate the concept of earthborn(e) democracy? First, rituals name practices of concerted action—shared attention as the pathway to shared intention—to constitute collective power. Second, as argued above, the relationship between attunement and emergence limns the doubled nature of being earthborn(e)—as being both carried by the earth and active bearers of earthly powers of regeneration. Third, the language of ritual shows the depth of democratic practices and desire, which are currently sublimated or asphyxiated by the incessant pressures of consumer capitalism and the shallow rituals of representative government and spectatorial politics. Fourth, as iterated practices of boundary drawing and contestation, rituals center questions of inclusion and community, and thereby hold the possibility of re-enchanting the world, as Federici suggests. Like the Blacktail Deer Dance of the Ktunaxa described in chapter 1, rituals reveal new horizons of community that can include the more-than-human.

The foregoing has been a relatively general discussion, yet rituals always take place and are embodied within specific locations, vernaculars, and cultures.[23] In the next section we lift up three examples of democratic practices of earthly entanglement to identify how attunement and emergence might appear in rituals of earthborn(e) democracy. In doing so, we foreground the particular places and participants carrying out rituals of democratic enactment. This shows the persistence and breadth of democratic experimentation, best understood as rituals of both attunement and emergence. In the face of the intertwined crises of democracy and ecology, we see recurrent aspirations to envision and practice alternative and more democratic forms of life, resonating with historical and psychic morphic fields of creative agency available to all earthly beings. Our examples stand as a rejoinder to the felt impasse and despair of the present moment.

"I AM NOT A NATION STATE": RITUALS OF INDIGENOUS REFUSAL

Our first example is drawn from the work of Leanne Betasamosake Simpson and her concepts of Indigenous resurgence, generative refusal, and grounded normativity. All these concepts and their attendant practices stem from close attention to a repressed and oppressed past for the sake of renewal and regeneration in the present. Simpson eloquently names radical practices of processual self-governance—what we see as rituals of democratic experimentation—in part by distinguishing these practices from relatively thin forms of engaging with settler colonial states. Simpson also shows the interrelationship between attunement and emergence through her account of decolonization as *biiskabiyang* or "a reemergence, an unfolding from the inside out."[24] Generative refusal, on our reading, exemplifies and embodies the democratic archetype of flight, which shows the depths of longing for collective freedom. Finally, Simpson's account of grounded normativity and "land as pedagogy" traces the ways in which rituals of self-governance in the face of chronic crises expand the boundaries of community by including and learning from the more-than-human world.

Simpson's *As We Have Always Done* reflects on Indigenous activism in the wake of the Idle No More protests that began in December 2012.[25] Her call to Indigenous resurgence is a reaction to witnessing how the protests addressed the Canadian settler state rather than regenerating Indigenous knowledge and relationships. Her observations of Idle No More are mixed. While encouraged by the scale and diversity of the protests and participants, Simpson concludes that the social movement's immediate success short-circuited the slower work of building alternative forms of life. "Social media gave us an opportunity to skip the hard work of being present, of doing ceremonies together, of sharing food, and of standing face-to-face with our people, even when we disagree."[26] On Simpson's assessment, Idle No More's quick rise and success came at the cost of building land-based processual self-governance.[27] Indigenous refusal is not just a naysaying to the settler state; it is a thousandfold yes-saying to community.

For Simpson, self-governance is collective, relational, processual, and expressive. Being Nishnaabeg for Simpson means that "everything is collective," and "being Nishnaabeg is being in relationships." The Nishnaabeg nation—the people—is "Kina Gchi Nishnaabeg-ogamig," the "place where we all live and work together."[28] The nation is "an ecology of relationships" that persists in the "absence of coercion, hierarchy, or authoritarian power."[29] Politics, then, for Simpson, is ongoing, relational work, rooted in place and community, that builds internal resources for resistance and refusal. The relational nature of these practices has intrinsic value because it restores and re-stories the Nishnaabeg nation.

In contrast to a vision of politics as episodic, transactional, and strategic, the work of politics for Simpson is processual and expressive of Nishnaabeg identity rooted in land-based relation-ships, a daily reweaving of life through rituals of collective self-fashioning. "Practices are politics. Processes are governance."[30] Practices such as hunting on the land, harvesting rice, telling and listening to Nishnaabeg stories, and doing ceremony all count as politics. Rituals of Nishnaabeg life are also and always practices of self-creation and governance. As Simpson puts it, "self-determined making" is the core of life "as a creative act."[31] "Governance was made every day," Simpson writes. "Leader-ship was embodied and acted out every day."[32] The future for Simpson thus emerges from living a different present, not merely dreaming alternate realities but creating them.[33] Poli-tics is expressive—requiring the articulation and embodiment of an alternative form of life—and generated through contin-ual processes and practices of resistance and resurgence. The daily work of imagining a Nishnaabeg reality is the daily prac-tice of living a Nishnaabeg life. For Simpson, the goal is not just to emphasize authority of elders but to proliferate new generations of "land-based, community-based intellectuals and cultural producers who are accountable to our nations and whose life is concerned with regeneration."[34]

The task is to build and continually rebuild the people through carrying forward the traditional knowledge and life-ways of the Nishnaabeg into the present, what Simpson calls a return to ourselves as a means of emerging from the shadow of settler colonialism. Simpson recognizes the seeming paradox of emergence through attunement. The "structural" basis of Nish-naabeg life *is* process and relationship; in our language it is the resonance field of a deeply democratic form of life that has been repressed but not vanquished under the settler colonial state. Nishnaabeg life is both past and present; resurgence is both an emergent practice of self-creation and assertion, but this emergence is enabled by a return and close attentive relationship to traditional stories, dreams, visions, and practices contained or held by living elders. Resurgence, then, is traditional *and* radical: as Simpson puts it, "resurgence is our original instruction."[35]

Resurgence is not only the embodied enactment of traditional knowledge passed across generations; it also draws practices of attunement to what Simpson refers to as the implicate order. The implicate order describes not some static "laws of nature" but rather a field of flux and transformation. As Sákéj Youngblood Henderson writes, "The spirits are never restricted to any particular embodiment, but generate transformations, the rearrangement of the mystery, the restructuring of the realms of the spirit and embodied spirits."[36] Attunement to the implicate order collapses past, present and future into a kairotic event of emergence or resurgence. Simpson looks back in order to look ahead; she prefaces many of her presentations with a narrative of "what our land used to look like," to offer an image of what has been lost, "not as a mourning of loss but as a way of living in an Nishnaabeg present . . . and as a way of positioning myself in relation to my ancestors and my relations."[37]

Above all, resurgence depends upon the one "no"—the refusal of the settler colonial state and its violence, which takes the form not only of territorial colonization and genocidal dispossession but also cultural imperialism and repression through compulsory assimilation and disappearance. Simpson's refusal joins a chorus of Indigenous theorists and practitioners who begin their accounts of Indigenous politics with refusals of the supposed parity of treaty relationships and the corollary legitimation of the settler colonial nation-state.[38] Simpson's idea of refusal elaborates Neil Roberts's idea of freedom as marronage, as a politics of isolation from the oppressive and encircling hegemony in order to create the conditions of emergence for a more autonomous community.[39] Roberts's key examples of freedom as marronage include runaway slave communities in the American Southeast, self-organized groups of Haitian peasants resisting the order of French colonialism, as well as interstitial spaces of retreat or refuge in the oppressive climate of antebellum America. For Simpson, refusal requires locating oneself in spatial constructs outside of settler colonialism as a mechanism to maintain dignity and self-sufficiency. Simpson refers to these as "tiny islands of Indigeneity" within the sea of "settler colonial spatialities."[40] These are "survivance" stories, to use Gerald Vizenor's term—stories of escaping into indigeneity.[41]

For Simpson, however, the language of resurgence resonates more than that of "survivance": "I refuse and I continue to generate."[42] Simpson's engagement with Roberts extends "freedom as marronage" by emphasizing the *generativity* of refusal. Flight is as much a flight *into* as a flight *from*. One "escapes into Indigeneity,"[43] through *biiskabiyang*, a flight into "processes of freedom and self-determination."[44] Flight is not just about renunciation; flight "shatters and refuses the containment of settler colonialism and inserts Indigenous presence."[45] Flight into indigeneity opens and affords new possibilities of collective life. For Simpson, this is a "flight into Nishnaabewin . . . a returning in the present to myself . . . an unfolding of a different present."[46]

Simpson's embrace of *kwe* as a method offers an example of this flight from the settler state's gender-colonial binary into indigenous resurgence.[47] *Kwe* denotes a spectrum of gender expression in the Nishnaabe language; *kwe* does not conform to a rigid gender binary nor is it essentialized. As a method, *kwe* combines emotional and intellectual knowledge "within the kinetics" of place-based practices. *Kwe* emphasizes the lived integration of theory and practice that shapes how one lives with oneself, others, and in the broader world. More than experiential, embodied, or individual knowledge, *kwe* is anchored in Nishnaabe intelligence and takes place within grounded normativity.

Simpson sees the process and practice of being Nishnaabeg as inherently connected to a relationship with the land and its more-than-human inhabitants. Grounded normativity, according to Simpson (writing with Glen Coulthard), is based on "deep reciprocity inherently informed by a deep relationship to place."[48] This is what Simpson refers to as "land as pedagogy." As she puts it, "*context is the curriculum* and the land, Aki, is the context."[49] Practices take place in contexts that give them meaning. Simpson notes that settlers can imitate or appropriate Indigenous knowledge, but they do so in a deterritoralizing fashion that misses the essence of grounded relationality, "the loving web of Nishnaabeg networks within which learning takes place."[50] Simpson summarizes land as pedagogy this way: "Nishnaabeg ways of knowing or generating knowledge, including visiting, ceremony, singing, dancing, storytelling, hunting, fishing, gathering, observing, reflecting, experimenting, visioning, dreaming, ricing, and sugaring."[51]

Land-based relationships are central to Nishnaabeg intelligence, ways of knowing and doing, indebted to habits of attention to, and imitation of, the more-than-human world: a multispecies "ecology of intimacy."[52] Simpson writes of the elders of Long Lake learning freedom from the eagles; agency from the maple trees who choose to share their sap or not; refusal and flight from members of the Hoof Clan; and a vision of migration from the eels who saved the Nishnaabeg when the settler colonists invaded.[53] To take one of these examples, Simpson describes how before the construction of the Trent-Severn locks, salmon similar to Atlantic salmon inhabited Lake Ontario. The salmon were respected within Nishnaabeg culture, and a convergence arose between how the Nishnaabeg and salmon organized, governed, and mobilized themselves. Simpson continues:

> Eels represented a similar convergence. Traveling through
> Lake Ontario from the Atlantic Ocean, eels again traveled
> as far north as Atlantic salmon into Stoney Lake. They were
> a tremendous source of protein; and in that sense were the
> base of the economy and the base of the nation. Their sheer
> numbers and ability to travel, adapt and celebrate the flux
> of the ecological context, the diversity of life and power of
> mass mobilization, impressed and informed Nishnaabeg
> thinkers. So much so that when one of our people had a
> vision for a mass migration from the Atlantic region to the
> Great Lakes, it resonated with the people because they

had already witnessed their relatives completing a similar journey.[54]

The mobilization inspired by the eels saved the Nishnaabeg from utter annihilation when settler colonists arrived because they, like the eels, had spread themselves around the Lake Ontario region. "This was part of the political strategy of our ancestors," Simpson observes.[55] Simpson's story of the eels highlights the close link between the land as context and practice. To practice is to be involved and invested in space and territory: "You need to take your body onto the land and do it. Get a practice."[56] The ecology of intimacy that Simpson describes is a set of ritualistic practices of drawing and redrawing the boundaries of a learning community, rooted in place and territory as a necessary means of revisioning.

Simpson's vision and practice of being Nishnaabeg partakes of the four dimensions of ritual described above: concerted action to constitute collective power ("I am not a nation state,"[57] and the resurgent Nishnaabeg community); the marriage of attunement and emergence (attention to the more-than-human world to inspirit *survivance*); archetypal resonance with a deep past that is not past (refusal as generative); and the creative drawing and redrawing of the boundaries of community to acknowledge earthly entanglements such that humans can learn from the more-than-human world (maples, salmon, and eels). Simpson helps us to articulate a politics of earthborn(e) democracy.

Simpson's account of Nishnaabeg is also deeply earthborn(e): carried by the earth (i.e., land as pedagogy) and emerging from creative, relational practices among humans and nonhumans (*biiskabiyang*, or creative resurgence). Although Simpson does not use the language of morphic resonance,[58] she still keys into how past, present, and future commingle within a broader field that she calls the implicate order, an order continuously influenced and shaped by the accreted actions and wisdom coincident with being Nishnaabeg. Moreover, while Simpson does not draw on the language of the archetypes, her depiction of refusal traces what we call the democratic archetype of flight, an archetype not limited to the Nishnaabeg tradition (e.g., Roberts' *marronage*) but a broader field of the human and more-than-human world (e.g. the eels' resonant pattern of exodus around the waterways of Ontario). Simpson powerfully orients the archetypal politics of flight through a practice of attending to and acknowledging earthly entanglements.

While Simpson rarely speaks in the language of democracy, she offers a vision of deeply and radical democratic practice consonant with being earthborn(e). Simpson's account of Nishnaabeg resurgence echoes our basic understanding of democracy as the aspiration for cooperation across difference in the name of collective freedom, which involves the exercise of power from within entangled webs of interdependent relations with the earth, much as Simpson illustrates how Nishnaabeg resurgence must take place in and with the land and all its inhabitants. The specific embodiment of earthborn(e) democracy by the Nishnaabeg cannot be directly imitated; it exists only for the Nishnaabeg on their territory. That said, the example can inspire generative refusal in the name of earthborn(e) democracy elsewhere and in other ways. While the pedagogy of being Nishnaabeg cannot be transported to other contexts without distortion, its very resurgence and survivance reveal contours of possibility for being otherwise—seeds of a thousand yeses.

"LEARNING TO BE DEMOCRATIC": RITUALS IN COOPERATION JACKSON

Our second example is drawn from the radical eco-socialist organization Cooperation Jackson, located in Jackson, Mississippi. Cooperation Jackson constitutes collective power through a proliferation of radical democratic experiments, most notably through cooperative institutions, people's assemblies, and grassroots organizing efforts to gain electoral power in Jackson. Cooperation Jackson also attunes to historical and ecological contexts, drawing upon the tradition of Black nationalism and the history of Black cooperatives to create an emergent regenerative community that builds autonomous political power. Through these efforts, Cooperation Jackson exemplifies what we call the democratic archetype of sociality by attuning to resonant fields of mutual aid and cooperation as ways to deepen democracy. Similar to Simpson, Cooperation Jackson recognizes that rituals of world-making can and must redraw boundaries of human and more-than-human communities, a process enabled by their evolving eco-socialist vision, which ultimately aims to revise the maps of political identity and membership of not just the Jackson region but also the world.

Cooperation Jackson emerged from experiences in the wake of Hurricane Katrina, when efforts organized by the New Afrikan People's Organization (NAPO) and Malcolm X Grassroots Movement (MXGM) to provide aid to displaced survivors brought organizers up against the reality of the state's abandonment of poor and Black people in the Gulf region. Before Hurricane Katrina, members of NAPO and MXGM had begun conversations that led to Cooperation Jackson; the experience of the state's abandonment galvanized these discussions. Between 2004 and 2010, NAPO and MXGM developed the Jackson-Kush plan, of which Cooperation Jackson was the key vehicle for creating a solidarity economy and advancing the struggle for economic democracy.[59] The Jackson-Kush plan has three fundamental components: (1) building People's Assemblies; (2) building a network of progressive political candidates; and (3) building a broad-based solidarity economy. People's Assemblies allow ordinary people to practice democracy by empowering them to make direct decisions about the community (not simply in the electoral field). The broad-based solidarity economy consists of a community land trust to purchase properties in west Jackson, interrelated worker-owned cooperatives ("Green worker co-ops") aimed at creating a regenerative local economy, plans for housing cooperatives in Jackson, community savings and investing programs, tool-lending and time-banking, alternative currencies, and other initiatives. Cooperation Jackson has also succeeded in electing candidates to a variety of municipal offices, including two different mayorships, in Jackson. These three fundamental components are still informing the ongoing work of Cooperation Jackson.[60]

People's Assemblies offer the most fully realized component of Cooperation Jackson's democratic practice. They gather people together to identify and address their shared concerns. People's Assemblies can take two forms. One is a Constituent Assembly, which is a representative body that relies on continual outreach to ensure its legitimacy and proper functioning. The second form of People's Assemblies is the Mass Assembly, which forms during moments of crisis. Defined as constituting one-fifth of the total population of a geographic area, the Mass Assembly exists to address and channel decision-making, such as when the People's Platform was under threat after Mayor Chowke Lumumba's untimely death early in his first term.[61] People's Assemblies played a key role in crafting the vision of the Jackson-Kush Plan and building power to support the passage of a citywide 1 percent sales tax to repair Jackson's outdated infrastructure.

People's Assemblies are both strategic and expressive—instrumentally and intrinsically valuable. Kali Akuno, cofounder and codirector of Cooperation Jackson, theorizes a People's Assembly as an event, process, and institution.[62] As an event, a People's Assembly convenes the people to engage pressing issues. As a process, it persists through standing working groups and committees. As an institution, it creates a social counterweight to conventional political institutions and elected officials, one half of a "dual-power" strategy in which Cooperation Jackson seeks to create power in both government and the people.[63] A People's Assembly is a forum where participants develop firsthand experience in democratic processes and the skills required to exercise power with others.

One of the central elements of democratic experimentation in Jackson is the intentional development of a variety of cooperative economic institutions. Cooperation Jackson's cooperatives, ideally, create "a model in which people can engage in a process of learning to be democratic with each other."[64] Cooperatives organize businesses and social organizations around democratic principles where all worker-owners have a vote in making key decisions. Cooperation Jackson started cooperatives for farmers growing food (Freedom Farms, a worker-owned farming cooperative), a cafe to sell that food (Nubia's Place Cafe in Jackson), and composting cooperatives to process waste from the cafe.[65] According to the organizers of these cooperatives, worker-owners developed and practiced key democratic principles such as accountability systems, deliberative processes, and participatory budgeting and planning in lieu of conventional hierarchical organization, where decision-making lies in the hands of bosses. Rituals of cooperation habituate participants to trust one another, break down individualism and narrow ideas of self-interest, and hierarchies centered in the model of capitalist production and consumption.

Cooperation Jackson's cooperative model has emerged through attunement to a deep tradition of Black cooperatives and mutual aid in the American south. Agricultural cooperatives have long been a feature of Black farming communities; formerly enslaved workers pooled resources to purchase and farm land in common, starting in the Reconstruction period. During Jim Crow, Black cooperatives grew out of necessity; white-owned businesses exploited Black customers or would not serve them. W. E. B. Du Bois embraced Black cooperatives as a strategy of economic *marronage,* a means of building independent Black power in the wake of Reconstruction's failure and the failure of white responsiveness to Black demands for equality.[66]

Alongside this history of cooperatives stands a history of insurgent political organizing to which Cooperation Jackson also attunes. Cooperation Jackson names the "spiritual or prayer circles" organized by enslaved peoples and the "Negro People's Conventions" that developed during Reconstruction as precursors to the People's Assemblies.[67] The Student Non-Violent Coordinating Committee (SNCC) sank deep roots in the region through its courageous organizing efforts during the freedom struggles of the 1960s.[68] The Mississippi Freedom Democratic Party contested the legitimacy of Mississippi's lily-white Democratic Party leadership and delegation to the 1964 Democratic National Convention. The example of Fannie Lou Hamer inspires several facets of Cooperation Jackson's plan, from her initiation of a cooperative farm in Sunflower County, Mississippi, to her strong-willed engagement with the formal political system, and above all to her democratic insistence on collective freedom as both a universal ideal and a practicable reality.

Cooperation Jackson has also emerged from attunement to the ecological entanglements of the Jackson-Kush region. As Akuno observes, Mississippi has, like most of the Deep South, developed "as a settler-colonial state" through extraction of natural resources such as "timber for colonial and antebellum ship building" and "cotton, tobacco, sugarcane, and rice."[69] Cooperation Jackson seeks to create "new norms" to repair the damage done to ecosystems and "regenerate the bounty of life" on the planet,[70] breaking from patterns of human and nonhuman exploitation. A regenerative economy is more attuned to ecological interdependence as it begins from an assumption of mutualism and cooperation with the more-than-human world as opposed to the mastery or control within the plantation model of capitalist development.

These elements of attunement allow an emergent politics that integrates Mississippi's institutional, historical, and ecological contexts in a wholly new way. *Regeneration* for Cooperation Jackson thus functions like resurgence for Simpson, holding together both attunement and emergence: both draw on generational inheritances to regenerate what has come before into new political forms of assembly and cooperation. Unlike Simpson, who emphasizes the continuity of what "we have always done," Cooperation Jackson pieces together precursors to anchor novel practices and institutions. People's Assemblies, for instance, borrow from Venezuelan communalism,[71] yet inform this institution with local historical and political content. These nascent institutional bodies, moreover, seek to cultivate the emergence of new embodied habits and dispositions.

Mutual aid as an orientation and set of practices forms the keystone of Cooperation Jackson's organizing. The mutual aid ethos emerges from contexts of crisis as a strategy necessary for survival in the face of anti-Black violence, yet it also points beyond such contexts toward affirmative practices of care and cooperation. Cooperation Jackson develops mutual aid from its origins in social life to institutions from neighborhood to city and beyond. Economic democracy and socialism come "from below" through mutualistic practices that can both provide spaces for democratic participation and check entrenched institutional power.[72] This reflects a deep democratic faith, one that takes explicit form in the "Deepening Democracy" campaign Cooperation Jackson also spearheaded, which organized low- and moderate-income communities around food security and health.[73]

In the face of the 2022 water crisis afflicting Jackson, Cooperation Jackson organized mutual-aid networks to provide water to residents. Cooperation Jackson also launched a water sovereignty initiative in October 2022, which sought to organize citizens around modernizing the city's water system. Cooperation Jackson articulated demands to maintain democratic control of a new system built primarily by local contractors and workers. While facing regulatory roadblocks, initiatives like this one affirm the democratic capacity to express power. Cooperation Jackson also advocated for increasing home- and community-based water and energy resources to sustain these mutual aid networks going forward.[74]

The eco-socialist vision of Cooperation Jackson proceeds from an appreciation of human and nonhuman entanglement and interdependence. In this vision, to borrow from Kimmerer, "the land is the one with the power." Cooperation Jackson owes some of this to the slogan of the Black nationalist movement to "Free the Land."[75] This call comes from the demands of the New Afrikan Party for reparations for slavery from the federal government; the group planned to use those reparations to establish a sovereign territory across the Black majority states of the American south (South Carolina, Georgia, Alabama,

Mississippi, and Louisiana). This territorial politics concerns not just possession of land but also learning from it. Black freedom has been intimated and enabled by attentive knowledge of, and developed with, the land. For example, as J. T. Roane puts it, the ecological interstices of plantation life, "including the trees, a range of plant life, fish, deer, rogue herds of cattle, feral hogs, snakes, rabbits, bears, turtles, and wolves, as sources of shelter, food, danger, connection, and information, served as the basis for intergenerational knowledge transfers that could be enacted through intimacies with place as well as across dissolution through forced location."[76]

The close relationship between freedom and the earth is perhaps best illustrated by a story told about the time when future mayor of Jackson, Chokwe Lumumba, and other early organizers of the Republic of New Afrika came to Mississippi from Detroit to create a new community.[77] In March 1971, a group of 500 women, children, and elders went to celebrate on their newly purchased land and were confronted by a blockade of local white residents, including the same law enforcement officers responsible for the recent Jackson State murders. The officers tried to prevent them from celebrating, declaring, "N———s, we're not going to have a land celebration today." The threat of violence was palpable, as both groups were armed. The group with Lumumba began to pray and after some time, the obstructing group parted. The New Afrikans went to their land and began to eat its dirt in celebration and gratitude. As Lumumba remembered it, "people started eating the dirt and that's where that slogan came from—Free The Land."[78]

Cooperation Jackson's practice of cooperative democratic politics partakes of the four dimensions of ritual described above: concerted action to constitute collective power (People's Assemblies and cooperative economic democracy); the marriage of attunement and emergence (tapping historical, political, and ecological inheritances for synthetic and creative emergence); archetypal resonance with a deep past that is not past (of mutualism); and the creative drawing and redrawing of the boundaries of community to acknowledge earthly entanglements such that humans can learn from and include the more-than-human world (learning from and with the land). Cooperation Jackson helps us to articulate a politics of earthborn(e) democracy.

On our understanding, Cooperation Jackson's rituals are deeply earthborn(e): carried by the earth (e.g., free the land) and emerging from creative, relational practices among humans and nonhumans (e.g., regenerative economies for learning how to be democratic). These rituals resonate with deep histories and a collective unconscious of democratic practice taking forms of mutual aid, economic cooperation, and the concerted action of democratic assemblages. Mutuality instantiates what we call the democratic archetype of sociality and its structure of interdependent cooperation and affective belonging. Sociality names the transformative experimentation with community integral to Cooperation Jackson's democratic practices.

Democracy stands at the heart of Cooperation Jackson's example. As Brandon King, one of the founding members of Cooperation Jackson, has said, it offers "a model in which people can engage in a process of learning to be democratic with each other."[79] The account of ritual above helps to theorize the expansiveness of such learning: participants develop not just ideas but habits, dispositions, and orientations—shared attention becoming shared intention. Similar to Simpson's "land as pedagogy," the mutual aid of Cooperation Jackson's eco-socialism coalesces individuals into collectives capable of political freedom, both its responsibilities and its pleasures. This learning in turn builds political capacity—civic muscle—for the exercise of power. Unlike Simpson's example, however, Cooperation Jackson foregrounds the language of democracy: cooperation and mutual aid are concerned, at the most fundamental level, with building the power of the demos to do things together.

RITUALS IN BROAD-BASED ORGANIZING

Our third example is drawn from the broad-based organizing (BBO) tradition with special attention to organizing chronicled by Romand Coles in and around Flagstaff, Arizona. BBO constitutes collective power through a relational practice of politics grounded in people's interests and aspirations while developing civic skill sets for understanding power dynamics and how to build bridges across differences. BBO also attunes to local traditions and lifeways within the community—in particular faith communities—seeing these as the essential building blocks for emergent action. Through these efforts, BBO exemplifies what we call the democratic archetype of politicality by attuning to democratic resonance fields of coalition building, democratic leadership, and pragmatic politics. Although conceived in anthropocentric terms, the political rituals of BBO have been recently extended to welcome more-than-human communities as well as human ones, a process that continues the relationship building and receptivity at the core of the BBO project.

Here we focus our analysis of BBO through the recent account of organizing in the American southwest by Romand Coles, but to contextualize the innovations of these efforts, we first recount how BBO emerged in the twentieth century in the United States. Most histories of BBO trace its origins to Saul Alinsky's Back of the Yards Neighborhood Council (BYNC), founded on Chicago's southwest side in 1939. Alinsky formed BYNC to support union organizing in the nearby stockyards and to address the needs of the impoverished community. Employing militant tactics such as sit-downs and boycotts, the BYNC succeeded in winning many concessions from city hall to improve local services.[80] With the support of Bishop Bernard James Sheil and the philanthropist Marshall Field III, Alinsky founded the Industrial Areas Foundation (IAF) in 1940. For decades after, the IAF organized and trained other organizers to empower local communities against entrenched interests. This model involved working with existing social institutions (churches, block clubs, small businesses, etc.) and training local leaders to articulate and defend their communities' interests.

Although broadly successful in its early years, the Alinsky model of community organizing was nevertheless used as a basis of exclusion to reinforce racial hierarchies and ethnic divisions. Upon Alinsky's death, this prompted Edward Chambers to adapt the model to include bridge building across cultural and religious differences and to enlist the substantive commitments of different faith communities to enlarge the basis of organizing to include not just group interests but also values.[81] Chambers also formalized and extended the IAF's model, making it more sustainable through requiring multiyear commitments from dues-paying member organizations. These resources primarily went to hiring and training professional organizers to lead initiatives in member organizations' communities.

These organizers teach local community leaders how to organize, through practices such as one-on-one relational meetings, house meetings, accountability sessions with elected leaders, and Mass Assemblies. A typical campaign includes hundreds of one-on-one meetings, which provide the means of identifying the community's most salient concerns while also building up the capacities for listening, expression, and receptivity—seen by IAF as essential political skills, best cultivated in intimate environments of exploration and attention.[82] These meetings can help weave and reweave the fabric of trust across differences as people come to know each other. In the IAF model, each organization also holds house meetings of about ten persons, building on the one-on-one meetings, and leading to even larger mass meetings convening all member organizations from a given community. It is in these mass meetings that the full power of the BBO approach becomes palpable and allows organizers to "turn the tables" on public officials who are invited into a public space they do not control (as opposed to presiding over an official meeting, e.g.).

IAF's accountability session exemplifies how BBO creates and sustains collective power. Jeffrey Stout describes the "rites" that form such sessions as ones of "solidarity, commitment, and mourning."[83] Officials and candidates gather in the community, organization leaders set the agenda, speakers from the community tell stories to illustrate the issues and their importance, leaders then lay out the organization's proposal and ask the officials to publicly declare yes or no on their agreement with those proposals. As Stout writes, "A politician who begins a stump speech quickly discovers that his or her microphone will simply be turned off."[84]

In these accountability sessions, communities create solidarity by coming together around shared values and experiencing shared power in holding elites accountable. As a rite of commitment, these sessions also force officials to commit to the values underlying these communities' proposals, binding these officials and communities together to a shared project. Yet these are also rites of mourning because they confront the losses these communities sustain, losses that produce anger and grief both felt and mobilized by the communities. The rites of accountability sessions illustrate how the BBO's relational practice of politics grounded in people's interests and aspirations creates collective power for the otherwise unorganized and marginalized.

The relationship building at the core of BBO's approach allows for attunement to both the traditions of a place and the capacities for power latent within individuals and communities. For Alinsky, local traditions are the "flesh and blood" of the community.[85] The first stage therefore is to engage with these traditions, which are reflected in the values and priorities of community organizations. It is impossible to overstate the importance of knowing the traditions of the people one is tasked with organizing, Alinsky asserts. "Start with the people, their traditions," Alinsky wrote.[86] "Just as knowledge of the terrain is of the utmost importance for military tactics in actual warfare, so too is the knowledge, the full understanding and appreciation of the power of local traditions. The first maxim in conflict tactics to all leaders of People's Organizations is that the tradition is the terrain."[87]

Tradition provides the terrain on which to begin, but BBO also foregrounds analysis of power dynamics that structure this terrain. Accountability sessions, therefore, provide crucial events for surfacing these power relations and rebalancing them through the exercise of an organized community's power. As Stout observes, in large, pluralistic societies governed by representative institutions, popular power is inherently dispersed and the convergent interests of elites means that accountability is a perpetual challenge. This challenge requires communities to build bridges across differences and thus address the relative weakness created by dispersal. Bridge building begins by identifying self-interest within each community organization, the articulation of which are large gatherings that allow for the identification of overlapping interests. As Stout puts it, "Member groups saw the formation of alliances as essential to actually changing things."[88] This insight also has the additional effect of shifting groups to more flexible self-understandings and more reflexivity about their values.

One of the key mechanisms of building democratic power for BBO organizers is to cultivate local leadership. Local leaders, according to Stout, emerge organically through practices of attention to whose voices carry weight within the community. In some cases, paid organizers identify and name how individuals are already inhabiting this role, even if those individuals are themselves unconscious of their authority and potential for leadership. By attuning to these oftentimes latent capacities, BBO organizers create the conditions for sustained collective action. Stout recounts the story of Carmen Anaya. She never learned English but would often be the major speaker at accountability sessions facing down then-governor of Texas, Mark White. As Stout recounts, quoting a community leader: "[Carmen] would put her hand on her hip and she would kinda shake her finger. She would be speaking Spanish to Mark White and he wouldn't know a word, but he was afraid to look away. So he would be looking intently at her, and she would be going like this [wagging her finger]." On one such occasion White is reported to have said, "I don't know what you're saying but I know I'd better say yes."[89]

BBO attunes to the capacities of leaders like Carmen Anaya, drawing them into public spaces to help coalesce collective power. For Coles, this reflects an even deeper inheritance within the life of the species. Coles describes the relationship between grassroots organizing and the neurological processes of intercorporeal resonance made possible by mirror neurons. Mirror neurons are a key part of human morphology that allow humans to attune to the emotional states of others and resonate with those states. Coles quotes the neuroscientist Marco

Iacoboni, who writes, "mirror neurons put the self and other back together again . . . (and) remind us of primary intersubjectivity."[90] For the sociobiologist Sarah Hrdy, mirror neurons testify to the deep species history of "alloparenting," or the fact that childrearing was a community-wide task involving the presence of extended familial networks early in human history.[91] As Coles writes of BBO in the American Southwest, "Resonance is at the root of thingness in a most basic sense, insofar as resonance not only is what happens among, to, and in things, but also is constitutive of the very emergence of things."[92] We are wired for intersubjectivity as a result of this deep archetypal pattern of interaction.

Rooting in community traditions, local vernaculars, organic leadership, and our species capacity for intersubjective attunement occurs all in the name of emergent practices of democratic power. As Coles puts it, "receptive rooting" enables "responsive routing," which takes the form of "moving democracy" and "mobile stewardship" along with "a host of other receptive flows."[93] The relational work of BBO enables "emergent transformative possibilities."[94] For example, Coles's discussion of the Action Research Teams (ARTs) illustrates multilayered, relational work developed in Flagstaff, Arizona, and North Arizona University (NAU). ARTs consist of several tiers. First, a seminar at NAU introduces college students to theories of democracy and democratic education. Second, the college students are paired with local K-12 students to facilitate democratic relationship building, receptive dialogue amid differences, public expression, and collaborative action, among other activities. Third, this creates emergent relationships among the broader communities in which these students participate, from the Native American communities (primarily Dine and Hopi), from which many students come, to the NAU campus, where new courses and professorships were created.[95] "Democratic innovation" emerges.[96] The ARTs, for Coles, are one means of "co-creating a radical democratic resonance machine," testimony to the intertwinement of attunement and emergence.

Coles's examples of the ARTs points to BBO's distinctive rhizomatic politics. Broad-based organizing pursues the "evolution of selves and practices" by centering encounter and relationship as the central means of transformation. The breadth of this organizing comes through contagion: one-on-ones ramify into house meetings, which then extend through mass meetings and accountability sessions. What appears as scaling up is just as importantly a spreading out. Stout describes the twofold rationale of BBO along these lines: first, to mitigate the tendency of groups to organize around a single identity or issue, which keeps groups open to lateral connections with as many other groups as possible; and second, to build up coalitions with enough power to address issues that cannot be resolved by merely applying political pressure.[97] These coalitions maintain a protean flexibility by virtue of the kinds of living relational practices chronicled by Coles. ARTs, to return to that example, constitute a "radical democratic habitus" where democratic tending and "dynamic reciprocal freedom" can flourish.[98]

Although, as noted earlier, much of the language and practice of BBO is anthropocentric and focused on the issues facing human communities such as housing, public services, immigration, education, and the like, this model of organizing can extend beyond humanity. The IAF practice of power analysis can give way to more nuanced considerations of power as circulatory, which Coles brings to the relationships between humans and nonhumans such as the "river of corn" flowing in, around, and through the bodies of twenty-first-century Americans.[99] "The river of corn" refers to the relationship between corporate and state power in the form of government subsidies to carbon-intensive agriculture that supplies Americans with low-nutritional foods for mass consumption in the form of high-fructose corn syrup. Understanding the circulation of power in this way allows for organizers to situate themselves and to initiate new counterflows; this requires attuning not just to human interests and community traditions but the way in which these interests and traditions are entangled with the more-than-human world. One might need to get on all fours to envision a multispecies democracy, which would involve multiple life forms dynamically intertwined. Coles cites the example of Joel Salatin of Polyface Farms, who offers a multispecies practice of attunement. Instead of gazing at a field of grass—an abstraction—Salatin sees "an immense, dynamic, and fructiferous complexity of symbiotic relationships that is 'not within our making.'"[100] Concretely, this involves regenerative agricultural practices like sustainable harvest rotation and developing ecological co-relationships amongst the different species that make up the farm. One must "be drawn into the orbits of cow's lips, eyes, and tongues," in Coles's language, to facilitate the transition to this approach to sustainable agriculture.[102] In the organizing efforts at NAU and in Flagstaff, this broader practice of boundary redrawing inspired attention to the more than human elements of climate, geology and hydrology that are more than background to human projects of collective power.

Just as Stout refers to the practices of BBO as "rites," we also see these experiments in building democratic power in ritualistic terms. Rituals build shared intention (will) through practices of shared attention, concerting actions to constitute collective power. They root in and re-create traditions to facilitate emergent routings and new possibilities for collective life, marrying attunement and emergence. The basic structure of broad-based organizing pursues breadth and depth through its focus on relationship building across differences, and it heralds a possibility for bridging beyond the human to organize ecologically sensitive counter-flows.

Rituals of broad-based democracy have not, historically, been consciously earthborn(e). But just as the practice expanded from Alinsky's community organizing model to emphasize bridge building across differences and social divisions, so, too, can BBO expand its practices of power analysis and mobilization to include the dynamics of ecological entanglement, in which power is always an earthly, shared reality, and the relevant relationships of political life can never be restricted to humans alone. The relevant democratic archetype for understanding the work of BBO is that of politicality, which we define in the previous chapter as the capacity to negotiate and build power across differences of perspective and experience. Politicality, like all the other archetypes, is earthborn(e) in the sense that it reflects the species inheritance of interspecies mutualism (recall, e.g., the Following Deer story from chapter 1) from which humans have departed thanks to the myth of modernity in which humans are seen as the only relevant actor or agent. The modern myth is largely responsible for the "river of corn," among other pathological, anti-ecological mega-circulations, which require the proliferation of counter-flows of ecological democracy.

BBO's rituals center the *power* of the people in its democratic practices. Power is concerted action, as Hannah Arendt put it; action in concert comes through the iterated and dynamic elements that form BBO's panoply: one-on-ones, house meetings, Mass Assemblies, and accountability sessions. Action takes place among participants, community organizations, elected officials, and nonhuman actors in these and other places. Relationship building also centers participation in democratic practices—and intimates the possible pleasures and affects inspired by being and acting together with others (including nonhuman others, like Joel Salatin's cows). BBO holds together an emphasis on self-interest—as the starting point for political organization—and transformation of self, other, and world that can take place through engagement in the processes and practices (i.e., rituals) of broad-based organizing.

DEMOCRATIC PRACTICES OF EARTHLY ENTANGLEMENT: FROM RITUAL TO MYTH (AND BACK AGAIN)

Lest the specificity of the three foregoing examples intimates exclusive ways of earthborn(e) democracy, the rituals named above are only part of a proliferating politics of entanglement that is largely unintelligible from within the terms of the modern myth. Leanne Betasamosake Simpson's refusal offers one possible embodiment of the democratic archetype of flight, but there are many others. Indigenous refusals articulated by Glen Sean Coulthard and Audra Simpson resemble Simpson's, though with more emphasis on Indigenous sovereignty as crucial to resurgence. The politics of refusal also take non-Indigenous forms, such as in Bonnie Honig's feminist politics of refusal or Saidiya Hartman's Black feminist refusals. With both Honig and Hartman, refusal takes choral forms, where action in concert arises through call and response of women in flight.[102] Gloria Anzaldúa's spiritual activism, with its flight back to the self for repair and action with others, shows how the embodiments of the archetype of flight can assume more coalitional forms of being together in fugitivity. Anzaldúa's flight also illustrates how border identities can pursue flight as a democratic form.[103] Alexis Pauline Gumbs' Black feminist lessons from marine mammals exemplifies an interspecies embodiment of the democratic archetype of flight, opening pathways for learning from and being with nonhuman fugitives.[104] Likewise, Leanne Betasamosake Simpson observes the historical flight of the Hoof Clan from Nishnaabeg territory in response to conditions of overhunting and the Nishbaabeg's lack of gratitude.

Embodiments of the democratic archetype of sociality can also take many forms. The U.S. Populist agrarian movement in the nineteenth century was predicated on deep networks of mutual aid and cooperation that allowed the movement to persist and grow into the political force it became, in ways that still resonate in consumer and producer cooperatives across the country.[105] John Curl and Nathan Schneider have pointed to the persistence and presence of cooperatives in the U.S. economy as sites of democratic growth and expansion.[106] Gar Alperovitz has outlined community-based systems, such as participatory budgeting, to redistribute wealth and power to localities.[107] Fred Moten's concept of radical study illustrates sociality's world-making capacities in the "undercommons" of Black life.[108] Sociality can also arise outside the United States in contexts like Mondragon,[109] Venezuelan communalism,[110] and the Kurdish separatist organization of Rojava.[111] Deborah Rose Bird's work illustrates the social life of nonhuman animals,[112] which Anna Tsing also finds among radjah shelducks, eclectus parrots, and Waigeo brush turkeys.[113] Merlin Sheldrake's work on fungi also exemplifies the democratic archetype of sociality among his subjects: symbiosis is a metaphor that can unlock all the ways in which mutualism and noncompetition are mechanisms of survival for many species, including mycelia ("the wood wide web").[114] Sociality blurs the hard boundaries between individuals, paralleling recent discoveries in the microbial sciences that make it "hard to define the boundaries of an individual organism."[115]

Politicality as a democratic archetype appears in manifold forms in addition to the organizing across differences illustrated by our examples of BBO.[116] Recent legislation in New Zealand extending rights to waterways, and Ecuador's move to recognize the rights of nature in its constitution are examples of drawing and redrawing the boundaries of political community to acknowledge earthly entanglement.[117] "Permaculture for the

People" is a training program designed to introduce participants to system-based thinking and problem-solving through first-hand experience with regenerative agriculture techniques, water use, and carbon cycling that restore damaged ecologies and address food sovereignty.[118] Social movements such as the Movement for Black Lives (M4BL), counter the politics of despair through the development of political imagination and civic muscle, rooted in practices of inquiry and focused on pragmatic problem-solving.[119] Charlene Carruthers, former director of Black Youth Project 100, has advanced a Black feminist queer organizing lens, using intersectional analysis of interlocking oppressions, to build networks of power across significant differences.[120] In the United States, undocumented workers have led efforts to democratize unions from within and win better work conditions in meatpacking factories.[121]

Political practice need not limit itself to a single archetype. Moten's description of the Black Panthers, which lifts up their "preservation" of Black life, resonates with what we call the archetype of flight,[122] but the Panthers' emphasis on mutual aid and self-provisioning embodies the archetype of sociality at the same time. Lia Haro and Romand Coles's analysis of communities along the path of the underground railroad exemplifies how flight and sociality mutually support one another, with refusal (of slavery) supported by caretaking (of fugitive slaves).[123]

Some of the more complex, emergent examples of what we call earthborn(e) democracy resonate with all three democratic archetypes. Recall Haraway's Camille stories recounted in the introduction, which mixed flight, sociality, and politicality. Cooperation Humboldt, formed in 2017 and inspired by the efforts of Cooperation Jackson, offers an actual example. Cooperation Humboldt has partnered with the Wiyot tribe in California to build a "restorative economy" within the traditional Wiyot homelands of the area. The very fact that the Wiyot are once again inhabitants of their ancestral territory is the result of decades of political organizing that involved working with local businesses, organizations, and state and federal agencies. In 2019, the City of Eureka, California, returned 45 acres on Tuluwat Island to the members of the Wiyot tribe, which represented the first time in the history of the United States that a city government had ever given land back to its ancestral caretakers.[124] After the return of the land, the Wiyot tribe could complete the world-renewal ceremony that was interrupted by settler colonialism in 1860. After more than a century of flight and refusal, necessary to sustain the memory of a way of life, and surrounded by countless acts of mutual aid and cooperation, this process issued in the intense and ongoing political labor of building power and negotiation across differences in order to achieve a long-sought goal—a deeply resonant example for other struggles in other places.

We consider all these examples as blossoms from the rhizome of earthborn(e) democracy. Identifying their practices as rituals calls attention to how these democratic experiments orient participants around shared objects, relate them to one another and to something beyond the here and now, and shape common affects and emotions. Different rituals can result in different political subjectivities. Rituals resonant with the archetype of sociality, like Cooperation Jackson, for example, instill mutuality, care, and concern. By contrast, rituals attuned to the archetype of politicality, like those of BBO, begin from self-interest and the moral flexibility of "no permanent enemies, no permanent friends." Yet, as Cooperation Humboldt illustrates, though the embodiment of each of these democratic archetypes are functional in different circumstances, political communities develop the greatest potential for democratic world-making when they can draw on the full range of archetypal possibilities.

Democratic world-making is a question of ecology, and ecological flourishing is a democratic task. The examples detailed above demonstrate how democratic rituals nourish and are nourished by the fact of being earthborn(e). Rituals are predicated on capacities for self-governance that are elements in the morphic field of human species being. These capacities, in a deep sense, are earthly phenomena, even as they are held within a translocal field of memory (conscious and unconscious). The crisis of democracy reflects ecological impoverishment, both in the sense of the specific, desiccated, and increasingly lonely landscapes of the planet, but also in the sense of a diminished ability to attune to the full range of inheritable democratic gifts. The loss of democratic habitat—as both hospitable territory and holding environment—has weakened the resonance of multispecies cooperation, with detrimental effects for humans as well as the more-than-human world. On the contrary, this chapter has detailed democratic rituals for restoring and being restored by habitats conducive to earthly flourishing.

The democratic rituals of earthly entanglement make sense within the overarching myths of earthborn(e) democracy as described in previous chapters. Myths require rituals, and rituals embody and enact myth. The relevant myths narrate the capacity for democratic action and collective freedom among the earthborn(e). The myths, as we are trying to surface them here, counter the failing and unreflexive modern myths that embalm popular power within the danse macabre of electoral politics and consumer capitalism. This dying myth also alienates humans from the more-than-human world, pretending that power is control or dominance as opposed to being an emergent property of ecological entanglement.[125]

Like a nurse tree, the dying myths of modernity can also nourish the myths of earthborn(e) democracy. The twin crises of democracy and ecology point to the need for new stories, but as this book shows these stories already exist and are made real by the democratic rituals of earthly entanglement we elaborate and catalog here. Earthborn(e) democracy is an inheritance of the species, one we can step into and claim wherever we are located. Culture is built through "as if" rituals—the performance of values that posit and make a world in which those values are normative or constitutive.[126] As these rituals attest, the cultivation of earthborn(e) democracy is already underway. Through a dual-faced practice of attunement and emergence, these rituals prepare the ground for the blossoming of a thousand yeses, and the rhizome from which these flowers bloom persists within the waking and sleeping dreams of the species—and of the earth.

ACKNOWLEDGMENTS

THIS BOOK began nearly two decades ago, though we could never have anticipated its development at that time. We would like to acknowledge all the people who have helped us along the way. First and foremost, J. Peter Euben, advised each of us through our doctoral work at Duke University and whose example of playfulness, conviviality, creativity, and curiosity inspired and continues to serve as a lodestar in our teaching, writing, and living. Romand Coles was also among our first teachers, and his energetic, imaginative, and promiscuous mind is a model for intellectual growth and engagement; he gifted us more than he likely realized (before reading this book). To all our other teachers at Duke and elsewhere, we express enormous gratitude.

In the last two decades, we have regularly gathered together, in person and online, to engage in study. We're grateful for this practice of study for all it has meant for each of our own intellectual lives, not to mention the friendship that has grown and blossomed through this shared activity. This process has created an intellectual habitat—a holding environment—where we could safely explore, take risks, experiment, and dream wildly. It's no exaggeration to say that without this collaborative process and the environment it fostered this book would be inconceivable.

We're grateful to all who supported our study, both directly and indirectly, during these years. While each of us has benefitted from readers and interlocutors for our individual work, the three of us together would especially like to thank the following people: Laura Grattan, Alisa Kessel, Stefan Dolgert, P. J. Brendese, George Shulman, Elizabeth Markovits, Keally McBride, James Martel, Antonio Vázquez-Arroyo, Elisabeth Anker, Alyssa Battistoni, Cristina Beltrán, Rom Coles, Mina Suk, Sara Rushing, Michaele Ferguson, Ben McKean, Claire Snyder-Hall, and Jean-Paul Gagnon. We also thank Adriene Mischler, Benji, and Paul and Sommer Sobin for upleveling each of our days.

We are grateful to be working with Columbia University Press and the wonderful Wendy Lochner as well as her staff. We also acknowledge the thoughtful engagement with our manuscript from two anonymous reviewers, as well as audiences at the meetings of the Association for Political Theory, American Political Science Association, Western Political Science Association, and the Five College Political Science junior faculty workshop, where we were fortunate to present chapters in progress. Rom Coles, Molly Farneth, and George Shulman all read the complete manuscript prior to publication and gave us thoughtful and inspiring feedback, some of which we incorporated into the final version and some of which we continue to carry with us (in our netbags!).

Our institutions have supported this work in direct ways with research support: Bryn Mawr College, Mount Holyoke College, and Colorado State University. This support has allowed us to spend concentrated time together writing. Tom Schlosser and Marilyn Loveness also gave us a week in their house on the Olympic Peninsula, for which we are grateful, and Jen Severski and Jed Haupt graciously opened up their home in Leadville, Colorado, to us, where we drafted the first chapter. We also thank our families for supporting this time away from other duties as well as the countless hours of study during the previous decades.

Ring the bells that still can ring!

NOTES

INTRODUCTION

1. Elizabeth Kolbert, *The Sixth Extinction: An Unnatural History* (New York: Henry Holt, 2014).

2. Neil Roberts writes from within the democratic tradition as a critic (*Freedom as Marronage* [Chicago: University of Chicago Press, 2015]), as does Cristina Beltrán (*Cruelty as Citizenship* [Minneapolis: University of Minnesota Press, 2020]). See further our discussion in Ali Aslam, David McIvor, and Joel Schlosser, "Democratic Theory When Democracy Is Fugitive," *Democratic Theory* 6, no. 2 (Winter 2019): 27–40, as well as Anne Norton, *Wild Democracy* (Oxford: Oxford University Press, 2023) and Sylvia Wynter, "1492: A New World View," in *Race, Discourse, and the Origin of the Americas*, ed. Vera Lawrence Hyatt and Rex Nettleford (Washington, DC: Smithsonian Institution Press, 1995), 5–57. On "freedom dreams" within and beyond democracy, see Robin D. G. Kelley, *Freedom Dreams* (New York: Penguin, 2002).

3. As Elisabeth R. Anker writes, the "freedom" of liberal democracy is "climate destruction." Anker, *ugly freedoms* (Durham, NC: Duke University Press, 2022), 148. See also Timothy Mitchell, *Carbon Democracy* (New York: Verso, 2013).

4. "Crisis" holds its own narrative trajectory that we seek to challenge: the imagination of imminent collapse, the need for total solutions, and the empowerment of central authorities all create prejudice against the consideration of democratic alternatives. "Crisis" can also block alternatives, though, as Jared Margulies has argued about anxiety, it can also function to "signal" the political and economic conditions that need transforming: Margulies, "Political Ecology of Desire: Between Extinction, Anxiety, and Flourishing," *Environmental Humanities* 14, no. 2 (2022): 243. For philosophical arguments against democracy, including this one, see Jason Brennan, *Against Democracy* (Princeton, NJ: Princeton University Press, 2017). For an ecological argument against the sufficiency of nonviolent democratic organizing, see Andreas Malm, *How to Blow Up a Pipeline* (New York: Verso, 2020).

5. Geoff Mann and Joel Wainwright, *Climate Leviathan* (New York: Verso, 2020).

6. Josiah Ober, "On the Original Meaning of Democracy," *Constellations* 15, no. 1 (2008): 3.

7. Sheldon S. Wolin, *Democracy, Incorporated: Managed Democracy and the Specter of Inverted Totalitarianism* (Princeton, NJ: Princeton University Press, 2008).

8. Our understanding of being "born" is indebted to Hannah Arendt's concept of natality. See Arendt, *The Human Condition* (Chicago: University of Chicago Press, 1957), 8-9. We are also inspired by Silvia Federici's remark that "reproduction is not just about material needs but about collective memory and cultural symbols that give meaning to our life and nourish our struggles." See Federici, *Re-enchanting the World: Feminism and the Politics of the Commons* (New York: PM Press/Kairos, 2018), 5.

9. Our language of entanglement is inspired by William Connolly's "entangled humanism" (*The Fragility of Things* [Durham, NC: Duke University Press, 2013]), but goes further by bringing this entanglement beyond the human. In this way, the politics of entanglement we detail here resembles Arturo Escobar's "radical relationality," which he characterizes as "the fact that all entities that make up the world are so deeply interrelated that they have no intrinsic, separate existence by themselves" (*Pluriversal Politics: The Real and the Possible* [Durham, NC: Duke University Press, 2020], xiii). Philippe Descola's work also engages entanglement in ways that align with ours: Descola, *Beyond Nature and Culture*, trans. J. Lloyd (Chicago: University of Chicago Press, 2013). Recent work on

multispecies anthropology extends theories of entanglement even further. See, e.g., Eben Kirksey and Stefan Helmreich, "The Emergence of Multispecies Ethnography," *Cultural Anthropology* 25, no. 4 (2010): 545–576; Eben Kirksey, *Emergent Ecologies* (Durham, NC: Duke University Press, 2015); Thom van Dooren, *Flight Ways: Life and Loss at the Edge of Distinction* (New York: Columbia University Press, 2014); and Deborah Bird Rose, *Shimmer: Flying Fox Exuberance in Worlds of Peril* (Edinburgh: University of Edinburgh Press, 2022).

10. E.g., Zoe Todd's discussion of "fish pluralities" refers to the layered relationality, ways of knowing, and defining of boundaries, in her study of the Inuit community of Paulatuuq, Arctic Canada, and its codevelopment with the region's fish species. She observes of these relationships that "Indigenous epistemologies . . . are rooted in dynamic relationships between people and their world"; see Todd, "Fish Pluralities: Human-Animal Relations and Sites of Engagement in Paulatuuq, Arctic Canada," *Études/Inuit/Studies* 38, nos. 1–2 (2014): 218. See also Merlin Sheldrake, *Entangled Life: How Fungi Make Our Worlds, Change Our Minds, and Change Our Futures* (New York: Random House, 2021); and David Abram, *The Spell of the Sensuous* (New York: Vintage, 1996).

11. The modern myth of human omnipotence, which denies entanglement, is reflected in what Elizabeth A. Povinelli calls the "geo-ontopower" of the modern state to distinguish between life and nonlife, a judgment that is the foundation for the state's right to develop land for extractive purposes. See Elizabeth A. Povinelli, *Geontologies: A Requiem for Late Liberalism* (Durham, NC: Duke University Press, 2016). Ailton Krenak similarly describes modern institutions of the state and corporations ("corporate monsters") as having the status of unrecognized myths that cut "humanity off from its spiritual home." For Indigenous communities like his (the Krenak community), these institutions have been and are, in his words, "abuse dressed as reason"; see Krenak, *Ideas to Postpone the End of the World*, trans. Anthony Doyle (Toronto: Anansi International, 2020), 25. He contrasts the idea of the alienation of humanity with another narrative that is consonant with our concept of earthly entanglement: "For a long time, we have been alienated from the organism to which we belong—the earth. So much so that we begin to think of Earth and Humanity as two separate entities. I can't see anything on Earth that is not Earth. Everything I can think of is a part of Nature" (22).

12. By emphasizing *earthly* entanglement, we go further than "entangled humanism" as articulated in William Connolly, *Facing the Planetary:*

Entangled Humanism and the Politics of Swarming (Durham, NC: Duke University Press, 2017). We discuss Connolly's work in chapter 1.

13. See the critical exchange in *Contemporary Political Theory* for multiple takes on the visionary dimensions of political theorizing: Ali Aslam, David McIvor, and Joel Schlosser, "Critical Exchange: Visionary Political Theory," *Contemporary Political Theory*, DOI: 10.1057/s41296-023 -00627-3.

14. Our thinking on impasse has been deeply influenced by the work of George Shulman.

15. Jane Bennett and William Connolly both theorize earthly entanglement in terms that further articulate earthly politics beyond Bruno Latour and Donna Haraway. We discuss each of their work more in chapters 1 and 2. See also Timothy Morton, *Being Ecological* (Cambridge, MA: MIT Press, 2018); John Dryzek, *The Politics of the Earth* (Oxford: Oxford University Press, 1997); Sharon Krause, *Eco-Emancipation* (Princeton, NJ: Princeton University Press, 2023); David Schlosberg, *Defining Environmental Justice* (Oxford: Oxford University Press, 2007); and David Schlosberg and Romand Coles, "The New Environmentalism of Everyday Life: Sustainability, Material Flows, and Movements," *Contemporary Political Theory* 15, no. 2 (2016): 160–181.

16. Arendt, *Human Condition*.

17. Bruno Latour, *Down to Earth: Politics in the New Climate Regime*, trans. Catherine Porter (Medford, MA: Polity, 2018), 38.

18. Latour, *Down to Earth*, 41.

19. Latour, 42.

20. Donna Haraway, *Staying with the Trouble* (Durham, NC: Duke University Press, 2016), 55.

21. Haraway, *Staying with the Trouble*, 118.

22. Here is Haraway: "We are compost, not posthuman; we inhabit the humus-ities, not the humanities.... Critters—humans and not—become-with each other, compose and decompose each other, in every scale and register of time and stuff in sympoietic tangling, in ecological evolutionary developmental earthly worlding and unworlding." Haraway, *Staying with the Trouble*, 37.

23. "Sovereignty" as a concept runs counter to the theory of entanglement we forward here. For Schmitt, the sovereign is the one who decides the exception, yet all decisions under conditions of entanglement are

distributed among participating agents implying that sovereignty is a dangerous fiction.

24. Haraway, *Staying with the Trouble*, 248.

25. Haraway, 43.

26. Haraway, 43. Note that, for some, Haraway's Cthulhu and Camille stories raise questions about her lost militancy. See, e.g., Sophie Lewis, "Cthulhu Plays No Role for Me," *Viewpoint Magazine*, May 8, 2017, https://viewpointmag.com/2017/05/08/cthulhu-plays-no-role-for-me/.

27. In fairness to Latour, though, he has also written at length about what he calls an "assembly of species." See Bruno Latour, *Facing Gaia: Eight Lectures on the New Climatic Regime*, trans. Catherine Porter (Medford, MA: Polity, 2017).

28. Josiah Ober, *Athenian Legacies: Essays on the Politics of Going on Together* (Princeton, NJ: Princeton University Press, 2005).

29. The language of earthly flourishing comes from Joel Alden Schlosser, *Herodotus in the Anthropocene* (Chicago: University of Chicago Press, 2020).

30. See David Graeber, "There Never Was a West," in *Possibilities: Essays on Hierarchy, Rebellion, Desire* (Oakland, CA: AK Press, 2007), 329–374.

31. As also pointed out in Norton, *Wild Democracy*.

32. Although we use the language of crisis here, we also acknowledge the limitations of that framing insofar as it anticipates a moment of revolution or turning and thereby implies a revolutionary subject or actor, which overlooks the ways that metamorphosis is always already happening at a variety of timescales and through the actions of multiple, entangled agents. See J. K. Gibson-Graham, "Beyond Global vs. Local: Economic Politics Outside the Binary Frame," in *Geographies of Power: Placing Scale*, ed. Andrew Herod and Melissa W. Wright (Malden, MA: Blackwell, 2002), 25–60.

33. In ancient Greece, autochthony named a community's belief that it had always lived in the same territory. Judging from Aeschylus's early use of the term in *Agamemnon*, it seems likely, according to James Roy, that *autochthon* was established in the Greek vocabulary before the mid-fifth century BCE; Roy, "Autochthony in Ancient Greece," in *A Companion to Ethnicity in the Ancient Mediterranean*, ed. Jeremy McInterney (Hoboken, NJ: Wiley, 2014), 242. The word itself is a compound of *autos* (meaning "same" or "self") and *chthon* ("land," or "earth"). Herodotus uses

autochthon of the Arkadians and Kynourians to mean that they inhabit the same land they have held since antiquity. Vincent J. Rosivach has argued that this was the original meaning of the word; Rosivach, "Autochthony and the Athenians," *Classical Quarterly* 37, no. 2 (1987): 294–306.

34. Cf. Demetra Kasimis, *The Perpetual Immigrant and the Limits of Athenian Democracy* (Cambridge: Cambridge University Press, 2018).

35. We note here Michael Hanchard's important contribution to re-storying autochthony in ancient Greece as inaugural for "race thinking" and racial hierarchy in the modern nation-state (see Hanchard, *The Spectre of Race: How Discrimination Haunts Western Democracy* [Princeton, NJ: Princeton University Press, 2018]). The key distinction mythologized in ancient Athens for Hanchard is a blurring of ethnos and ethos, of peoplehood and practices. This clearly illustrates the persistent challenge of founding and sustaining egalitarian institutions across differences; "race thinking," as the heir to autochthony's exclusionary uses in ancient Athens, "solves" this challenge by creating racial hierarchies where one ethnos dominates all others. Hanchard also perceptively identifies contemporary authoritarian populists as "new autochthonists" motivated by a "mythos" of homogeneity founded on a "racial imaginary" (212). See also Jill Frank's response to Hanchard's interpretation of ancient Athens as the progenitor of ethno-national political inequality, which agrees with Hanchard while adding that ancient Athens also originated a critique of such inequality; Frank, "Athenian Democracy and Its Critics," *Ethnic and Racial Studies* 42, no. 8 (2019): 1306–1312.

36. Nicole Loraux, *The Children of Athena: Athenian Ideas of Citizenship and the Division Between the Sexes*, trans. Caroline Levine (Princeton, NJ: Princeton University Press, 1981).

37. On this point, see Elizabeth Irwin, "The Nothoi Come of Age? Illegitimate Sons and Political Unrest in Late Fifth-Century Athens," in *Minderheiten und Migration in der griechisch-römischen Welt: Politische, rechtliche, religiöse und kulturelle Aspekte*, ed. P. Sänger (Paderborn, Germany: Schöningh Wissenschaftsverlag), 75–112.

38. As Rosivach puts it, autochthony was "a vehicle for the expression of political, or more exactly ideological beliefs linked to Athenian democracy" ("Autochthony and the Athenians," 301). The democratic effects of autochthony varied with its political use. While Pericles's citizenship laws marked the sovereignty of the Athenian polis to exclude citizens, they

also leveled the hierarchies among elites and non-elites. "Even the lowliest citizen," Rosivach points out, "is superior, of nobler birth, than any non-citizen" (303).

39. Josine H. Blok, "Gentrifying Genealogy: On the Genesis of the Athenian Autochthony Myth," in *Antike Mythen: Medien, Transformationen, und Konstruckionen*, ed. Ueli Dill and Christine Wilde (Berlin: De Gruyter, 2009), 251–275.

40. Benjamin Isaac, *The Invention of Racism in Classical Antiquity* (Princeton, NJ: Princeton University Press, 2004), 132–133.

41. Roy, "Autochthony in Ancient Greece," 242.

42. Timothy Morton also pushes on this issue in his *Humankind: Solidarity with Nonhuman People* (London: Verso, 2017). See also Povinelli's vision of a multispecies demos in *Geontologies*, 118–143.

43. Language from Schlosser, *Herodotus in the Anthropocene*. See also Walter Mignolo's critical engagement with Schmitt, where Mignolo observes the eclipse of Schmitt's "nomos of the earth" and the emergence of a "third nomos" of the earth through reconstitution of Indigenous relations to and with one another and nonhumans. See Mignolo, *The Politics of Decolonial Investigations* (Durham, NC: Duke University Press, 2021), 483–530. Thanks to Sabeen Ahmed for this reference.

44. Latour writes, "Whereas Humans are defined as those who take the Earth, the Earthbound are *taken by it.*" Latour, *Down to Earth*, 251.

45. Gloria E. Anzaldúa, *A Light in the Dark/Luz en lo Oscuro* (Durham, NC: Duke University Press, 2015).

46. As Vine Deloria Jr. and Daniel Wildcat note, to be Indigenous means "to be of place," which Soren C. Larsen and Jay T. Johson elaborate as "a way of being and knowing . . . grounded in the agency of place to teach the responsibilities of land." Deloria and Wildcat, *Power and Place: Indian Education in America* (Golden, CO: Fulcrum Resources, 2001), 31; Larsen and Johnson, *Being Together in Place: Indigenous Coexistence in a More Than Human World* (Minneapolis: University of Minnesota Press, 2017), 3.

47. Robin Wall Kimmerer, *Braiding Sweetgrass* (Minneapolis: Milkweed Editions, 2015), 209.

48. Kimmerer, *Braiding Sweetgrass*, 7.

49. Kevin Bruyneel's *Settler Memory* argues that the erasure of Indigenous peoples from collective memory fosters an uncanny remembrance in popular imagination, cut off yet still accessible if not for ongoing disavowal of that knowledge. Michael Rogin further shows in *Fathers and Children*

that indigeneity and its associations with the land and other species were a disavowed shadow that both called for and justified settler expropriation and violence. Bruyneel, *Settler Memory: The Disavowal of Indigeneity and the Politics of Race in the United States* (Chapel Hill: University of North Carolina Press, 2021); Rogin, *Fathers and Children: Andrew Jackson and the Subjugation of the American Indian* (New York: Routledge, 1991).

50. Sheldon S. Wolin, *Politics and Vision*, exp. ed. (Princeton, NJ: Princeton University Press, 2004).

51. For an extended discussion of visionary political theory, see Aslam et al., "Critical Exchange."

52. Like Sheldon Wolin's epic theory, our visionary democratic theory is concerned with the whole political world, involving a new way of looking at the familiar world. Both modes of theory seek to break from habitual frames and framing, are creative, playful, and spontaneous. Our visionary theory is also informed by public concern and responses to a world in crisis.

53. As Eve Sedgwick argues, critique has not delivered on its promised breakthroughs; instead, critique tends to elaborate problems without seeing beyond them, metastasizing anxiety. Sedgwick calls for theory as a reparative mode of inquiry that summons a broader psychoanalytic framework. We affirm these reparative actions, but our visionary democratic theory also seeks to imagine a world where such repair is much less necessary. Critique needs repair, just like heroism needs attunement or awareness. See Sedgwick, *Touching Feeling: Affect, Pedagogy, Performativity* (Durham, NC: Duke University Press, 2002).

54. We take, e.g., Charles Mills's deracialized liberalism as exemplary in this respect: normative political theorizing offers powerful tools for calling a political order to account. See Mills, *The Racial Contract* (Ithaca, NY: Cornell University Press, 1997). Sharon Krause has usefully broadened this normative theorizing to consider nonhuman political actors as well. See Krause, "Politics Beyond Persons: Political Theory and the Non-human," *Political Theory* (2016), https://doi.org/10.1177/0090591716651516.

55. While Mills illustrates how norms can be leveraged against the very racist structure in which they were first articulated, normative theory presents too narrow a subject of theory, ignoring embodiment, history, and ecologies (to name a few factors). Moreover, normativity without a critical mode elevates a particular position to a universal norm: the silent background of human rights is the reasonable white male. As Sylvia Wynter

demonstrates, we must critically evaluate the categorical exclusions and complex entanglements of the human being prior to any normative theorizing. Normativity needs particularity, or granularity. See Wynter, "1492."

56. "Vision" should not exclude other sensorial attunements. See, e.g., Anatoli Ignatov's work on forms of listening in Ignatov, "African Orature as Ecophilosophy: Tuning In to the Voices of the Land," *Geohumanities* 2, no. 1 (2016): 76–91; and Ignatov, "The Earth as a Gift-Giving Ancestor: Nietzsche's Perspectivism and African Animism," *Political Theory* 45, no. 1 (February 2017): 52–75. These articles build on earlier work that emphasized the aesthetic's visual dimension (e.g., Ignatov, "Practices of Ecosensation: Opening Doors of Perception to the Nonhuman," *Theory and Event* 14, no. 2 [2011]).

1. PATHS NOT TAKEN:
RESONANT HISTORIES OF EARTHBORN(E) DEMOCRACY

The epigraphs for this chapter are from David Graeber and David Wengrow, *The Dawn of Everything* (New York: Farrar, Strauss and Giroux, 2021), 498 and 525; and Robin Wall Kimmerer, *Braiding Sweetgrass* (Minneapolis: Milkweed Editions, 2015), 263.

1. Sheldon S. Wolin, "Fugitive Democracy," *Constellations* 1 (1994): 11–25.
2. James C. Scott, *Seeing Like a State* (New Haven, CT: Yale University Press, 1998).
3. This point is detailed by Michel Foucault across his oeuvre but specifically in *Security, Territory, Population*, ed. Graham Burchell (New York: Palgrave, 2007).
4. David McIvor, "The Conscience of a Fugitive," *New Political Science* 38, no. 3 (2016): 411–427.
5. Wolin, "Fugitive Democracy," 347.
6. D. W. Winnicott inspires our discussion of holding. For Winnicott, the holding environment allows the infant to "have both an inside and the outside," to enable both "continuity of being" and a capacity for concern for the being of others; see Winnicott, *The Maturational Processes and the Facilitating Environment: Studies in the Theory of Emotional Development* (London: Karnac and the Institute of Psychoanalysis, 1990), 45–46. In terms of democracy, the holding environment denotes the context in which democratic subjects develop a sense of themselves as such and their

relationships to a common world. See also discussions by Bonnie Honig, *Public Things: Democracy in Disrepair* (New York: Fordham University Press, 2017); Joel Alden Schlosser, "Speaking Silence: Holding and the Democratic Arts of Mourning," in *The Democratic Arts of Mourning*, ed. A. Hirsch and D. McIvor (Lanham, MD: Lexington Books, 2019), 187–206; and David McIvor, *Mourning in America: Race and the Politics of Loss* (Ithaca, NY: Cornell University Press, 2016).

7. We also explore holding environments and democratic praxis through the language of auto- and allo-plasticity in Ali Aslam, David McIvor, and Joel Schlosser, "Democracy and the Unconscious," *Polity* 56, no. 1 (January 2024): 40–64.

8. Rupert Sheldrake cites Hans Spemann (1921), Alexander G. Gurwitsch (1922), and Paul Weiss (1923) as the first theorists of morphic resonance. See Hans Spemann, *Embryonic Development and Induction* (New Haven, CT: Yale University Press, 1938); Alexander G. Gurwitsch, "Uber den Begrlff des embryonalen Feldes," *Archiv für Entwicklungsmechanik der Organismen* 51 (1922): 388–415; and Paul A. Weiss, "Morphodynamische Feldtheorie und Genetik," *Zeitschrift für induktive Abstammungs- und Vererbungslehre 2* (supplement) (1928): 1567–1574.

9. Rupert Sheldrake, "The Extended Mind," *Quest*, July–August 2003, 1–6.

10. Rupert Sheldrake, *The Presence of the Past: Morphic Resonance and the Memory of Nature* (Toronto: Park Street Press, 2012), 3.

11. Sheldrake, *Presence of the Past*, 235.

12. This phenomenon resonates with William E. Connolly's discussions of swarming in, e.g., *The Fragility of Things* (Durham, NC: Duke University Press, 2013), and *Facing the Planetary: Entangled Humanism and the Politics of Swarming* (Durham, NC: Duke University Press, 2017).

13. Sheldrake, *Presence of the Past*, 436.

14. Sheldrake, 123.

15. Genetic accounts also miss heritability problems and evidence for epigenetics.

16. We describe this morphic field in terms of archetypes and the collective unconscious in chapter 2.

17. We borrow the language of freedom dreams from Robin D. G. Kelley, *Freedom Dreams* (New York: Penguin, 2002).

18. William E. Connolly, *Capitalism and Christianity, American Style* (Durham, NC: Duke University Press, 2008), 40.

19. Connolly's most recent book, *Climate Machines, Fascist Drives, and Truth* (Durham, NC: Duke University Press, 2019), brings this evangelical-neoliberal resonance machine to his explanation of climate denial in "The Anthropocene as Abstract Machine."

20. Connolly, *Fragility of Things*, 148.

21. Graeber and Wengrow, *Dawn of Everything*, 503 and 525. Subsequent citations to this book in this chapter appear parenthetically.

22. Murray Bookchin, *The Ecology of Freedom* (Chico, CA: AK Press, 1982).

23. Cf. James C. Scott, *Against the Grain* (New Haven, CT: Yale University Press, 2017).

24. C. L. R James, "Every Cook Can Govern. A Study of Democracy in Ancient Greece, Its Meaning for Today," *Correspondence* 2, no. 12 (June 1956): 1–20.

25. But we might resist this conclusion: that there's a shadowed anti-democracy always there. Graeber and Wengrow are too optimistic and progressive here—namely, in terms of their implicit dialectical materialism and their liberal faith that the facts will prevail.

26. Eduardo Viveiros de Castro, *The Relative Native: Essays on Indigenous Conceptual Worlds* (Chicago: HAU Press, 2015); Eduardo Kohn. *How Forests Think: Toward an Anthropology Beyond the Human* (Berkeley: University of California Press, 2013); Marisol de la Cadena, *Earth Beings: Ecologies of Practice Across Andean Worlds* (Durham, NC: Duke University Press, 2015); Zoe Todd, "Fish Pluralities: Human-Animal Relations and Sites of Engagement in Paulatuuq, Arctic Canada," *Études/Inuit/Studies* 38, nos. 1–2 (2014): 217–238; Soren C. Larsen and Jay T. Johnson, *Being Together in Place: Indigenous Coexistence in a More Than Human World* (Minneapolis: University of Minnesota Press, 2017).

27. Kimmerer, *Braiding Sweetgrass*, 236.

28. Kimmerer, 15.

29. Kimmerer, ix.

30. Kimmerer, 69. Like what we describe in chapter 2 as archetypal action, here Kimmerer describes a story that is acted out, not determining the particular action but giving a form for its iteration and articulation by the storytellers and auditors.

31. Walter Benjamin, "The Image of Proust." In *Illuminations*, trans. H. Zohn (New York: Schocken Books, 1968), 201–216.

32. Kimmerer's appreciation of the link between re-storying and ecological restoration gels with Candace Fujikane's effort to contrast Indigenous

narratives of abundance (concerning water and the nonhuman life it supports) with capitalist economies of scarcity as a way to contest the expansion of telescopes on the "wastelands" of Mauna Wakea's "barren" slopes, a volcano believed to be sacred by native Hawai'ians. See Fujikane, *Mapping Abundance for a Planetary Future* (Durham, NC: Duke University Press, 2021), 86–114.

33. Kimmerer, *Braiding Sweetgrass*, 179.

34. Kimmerer's description of distributed agency resonates with Jane Bennett's account of vibrant materialism, which we discuss more in chapter 2.

35. Kimmerer, *Braiding Sweetgrass*, 183.

36. Jessica Hernandez in *Fresh Banana Leaves* argues that restoration requires asking permission and relationship building with nonhumans. Hernandez, *Fresh Banana Leaves: Healing Indigenous Landscapes Through Indigenous Science* (New York: Penguin Random House, 2022).

37. Kimmerer, *Braiding Sweetgrass*, 304.

38. Kimmerer, 214.

39. Kimmerer, 246.

40. Kimmerer, 319.

41. Kimmerer, 264.

42. Kimmerer, 166.

43. Kimmerer, 184.

44. Kimmerer, 169.

45. Kimmerer, 168.

46. Kimmerer, 172.

47. Timothy Morton, *Being Ecological* (Cambridge, MA: MIT Press, 2018).

48. Although Kimmerer does not elaborate, this phrase—that the land is the one with the power—evinces the decolonial edge of her critique. As Max Liboiron writes, "Colonialism, first, foremost, and always, is about *Land*." Liboiron, *Pollution Is Colonialism* (Durham, NC: Duke University Press, 2021), 10; emphasis in the original.

49. Kimmerer, *Braiding Sweetgrass*, 169. A concern for regenerating and preserving democratic capacities must also involve confronting ongoing practices of settler colonialism and insisting on land repatriation in keeping with the demands of many Indigenous communities. Here Kimmerer is not explicit about what refusals the founding of Maple Nation, e.g., might entail. On the need for refusal and the dangers of state recognition, see Glen Sean Coulthard, *Red Skin, White Masks: Rejecting the Colonial*

Politics of Recognition (Minneapolis: University of Minnesota Press, 2014). See also the work of Leanne Betasamosake Simpson, which we discuss in chapter 3. Paige West's work on Papua New Guinea illustrates strong reasons for suspicions around environmentalism's cloaking colonialism: West, *Conservation Is Our Government Now: The Politics of Ecology in Papua New Guinea* (Durham, NC: Duke University Press, 2006), and West, *Dispossession and the Environment: Rhetoric and Inequality in Papua New Guinea* (New York: Columbia University Press, 2016).

50. Brian Noble, "Treaty Ecologies: With Persons, People, Animals, and the Land," in *Resurgence and Reconciliation: Indigenous-Settler Relations and Earth Teachings*, ed. Michael Asch, John Borrows, and James Tully (Toronto: University of Toronto Press, 2018), 315–342.

51. Noble's story aligns with a claim about how hunting reflects the dynamic transformation of Indigenous morality and "tradition." According to Nicholas James Reo and Kyle Whyte, tradition in Indigenous communities is dynamic because "people constantly rethink and transform traditional practices, often for pragmatic reasons when they face changing circumstances and new challenges." Reo and Whyte, "Hunting and Morality as Elements of Traditional Ecological Knowledge," *Human Ecology* (December 2010), http://dx.doi.org/10.2139/ssrn.1739805.

52. Noble, "Treaty Ecologies," 318.

53. See James Tully, *Strange Multiplicity: Constitutionalism in the Age of Diversity* (Cambridge: Cambridge University Press, 1995).

54. Noble, "Treaty Ecologies," 322.

55. See, further, Patty Krawec, *Becoming Kin: An Indigenous Call to Unforgetting the Past and Reimagining Our Future* (Minneapolis: Broadleaf Books, 2022); and Donna Haraway on kin-making in *Staying with the Trouble* (Durham, NC: Duke University Press, 2016).

56. Clark Wissler, *Mythology of the Blackfoot Indians*, Anthropological papers of the American Museum of Natural History, vol. 2, pt. 1 (New York: American Museum of Natural History, 1908), 157–158.

57. Norman O. Brown, *Love's Body* (Berkeley: University of California Press, 1966), 206

58. See Anne Norton on the "anarchic core" of democracy; Norton, *Wild Democracy* (Oxford: Oxford University Press, 2023). See also Cedric Robinson, *Terms of Order: Political Science and the Myth of Leadership* (Chapel Hill: University of North Carolina Press, 2016).

2. THE EARTHBORN(E) UNCONSCIOUS
AND DEMOCRATIC ARCHETYPES

The epigraphs from this chapter are from Carl Jung, *Memories, Dreams, Reflections* (London: Vintage, 1989), 205–206; and Norman O. Brown, *Love's Body* (Berkeley: University of California Press, 1966), 214.

1. Max Horkheimer and Theodore Adorno, *Dialectic of Enlightenment: Philosophical Fragments*, trans. Edward Jephcott (Palo Alto, CA: Stanford University Press, 2002).
2. Adrian Parr, *Birth of a New Earth: The Radical Politics of Environmentalism* (New York: Columbia University Press, 2017), 171.
3. Parr, *Birth of a New Earth*, xx.
4. Amy Allen, *Critique on the Couch: Why Critical Theory Needs Psychoanalysis* (New York: Columbia University Press, 2020), 24.
5. Joel Whitebook, *Perversion and Utopia* (Cambridge, MA: MIT Press, 1996).
6. Carl Jung, "Archetypes of the Collective Unconscious." In *The Collected Works of C. G. Jung*, vol. 9, pt. 1, (London: Routledge, 1991), 4.
7. Jung, "Archetypes of the Collective Unconscious," 66.
8. Carl Jung, *The Portable Jung* (New York: Penguin, 1976), 65.
9. Jung, *Portable Jung*, 38.
10. Sigmund Freud, *The Interpretation of Dreams* (London: Penguin, 1983), 38; Freud, *Totem and Taboo* (London: Routledge, 2015), 157.
11. Jung, *Portable Jung*, 38.
12. Jung, 59.
13. Jung, 45.
14. Jung, 95.
15. Although Jung also notes that it can also lead to the "sterility and monotony of those who have divested themselves of their egos"; Jung, 95.
16. Jung, 44
17. Jung, 43
18. Jung, 43.
19. Jung, "Archetypes of the Collective Unconscious," 11
20. Jung, 13.
21. "The archetype is essentially an unconscious content that is altered by becoming conscious and by being perceived, and it takes its colour from the individual consciousness in which it happens to appear"; Jung, 5.
22. Jung, *Portable Jung*, 31.

23. Jung, 60.
24. "The archetypes are simply the forms which the instincts assume. From the living fountain of instinct flows everything that is creative; hence the unconscious is not merely conditioned by history, but is the very source of the creative impulse. It is like Nature herself—prodigiously conservative, and yet transcending her own historical conditions in her acts of creation"; Jung, 44.
25. See Robert Bly, *A Little Book on the Human Shadow* (New York: Harper-Collins, 1998); and Bly, *Iron John: A Book About Men* (Cambridge, MA: Da Capo Press, 2013).
26. Demaris Wehr, *Jung and Feminism: Liberating Archetypes* (London, Routledge: 1987), 11.
27. Susan Rowland, *Jung: A Feminist Revision* (London: Polity, 2002), 80.
28. Jung, *Portable Jung*, 44.
29. Rowland, *Jung*, 92–93.
30. This also dovetails with Rupert Sheldrake's account of morphic resonance, discussed in chapter 1.
31. Jung, *Portable Jung*, 81.
32. William Ophuls, *Plato's Revenge* (Cambridge, MA: MIT Press, 2011), 71.
33. Ophuls, *Plato's Revenge*, 84.
34. Ophuls, 71.
35. Ophuls, 97.
36. Ophuls, 196.
37. Ophuls, 133.
38. Ophuls, 135.
39. Ophuls, 127.
40. Ophuls, 158.
41. Noelle McAfee, *Fear of Breakdown: Politics and Psychoanalysis* (New York: Columbia University Press, 2019), 13.
42. McAfee, *Fear of Breakdown*, 40 and 13.
43. McAfee, 9 and 40.
44. Felix Guattari, *The Guattari Reader*, ed. Gary Genosko (Cambridge, MA: Blackwell, 1996), 137.
45. Guattari, *Guattari Reader*, 77.
46. Guattari, 78.
47. Guattari, 86.
48. Guattari, 88.
49. Franco Berardi, *The Third Unconscious* (London: Verso, 2021), 57.

50. Guattari, *Guattari Reader*, 132.

51. Felix Guattari, *The Three Ecologies* (London: Athlone Press, 2000), 34.

52. Cf. Rupert Sheldrake, *The Presence of the Past: Morphic Resonance and the Memory of Nature* (Toronto: Park Street Press, 2012).

53. Cf. Martin Breaugh, *The Plebeian Experience* (New York: Columbia University Press, 2007).

54. Cf. James Scott, *The Art of Not Being Governed* (New Haven, CT: Yale University Press, 2010).

55. David Graeber and David Wengrow, *The Dawn of Everything* (New York: Farrar, Strauss and Giroux, 2021), 362.

56. Graeber and Wengrow, *Dawn of Everything*, 45.

57. Graeber and Wengrow, 454.

58. Graeber and Wengrow, 455.

59. Cf. James C. Scott, *Domination and the Arts of Resistance* (New Haven, CT: Yale University Press, 1992).

60. See John Gaventa, *Power and Powerlessness: Quiescence and Rebellion in an Appalachian Valley* (Champagne: University of Illinois Press, 1982).

61. Guattari, *Guattari Reader*, 137.

62. Guattari, 125.

63. Guattari, 128. "The aim is to reaffirm, stronger than ever, the right to singularity, to the freedom of the individual and collective creation, and the removal of technocratic conformism; the goal is to do away with the arrogance of all forms of postmodernism and to conjure up and call attention to the dangers inherent in the levelling out of all subjectivity that is being prompted in the wake of new technologies"; Guattari, *Guattari Reader*, 59.

64. Todd Meyers and Camille Robcis, "Jean Oury and Clinique de La Borde: A Conversation with Camille Robcis," *Somatosphere*, June 3, 2014, http://somatosphere.net/2014/jean-oury-and-clinique-de-la-borde-a-conversation-with-camille-robcis.html.

65. Robin Wall Kimmerer, *Braiding Sweetgrass* (Minneapolis: Milkweed Editions, 2015).

66. Josiah Ober, "On the Original Meaning of Democracy," *Constellations* 15, no. 1 (2008): 3–9.

67. The archetype is a resonance field that holds creative potentials for worldmaking. In chapter 3 we elaborate rituals that attune to the morphic fields of flight, sociality, and politicality.

68. Graeber and Wengrow, *Dawn of Everything*, 131.

69. Ophuls, *Plato's Revenge*, 196.

70. Ophuls, 35.
71. Ophuls, 164.
72. Ophuls, 151.
73. Kimmerer, *Braiding Sweetgrass*, 31.
74. Kimmerer, 31.
75. Kimmerer, 83.
76. Kimmerer, 185 and 195.
77. Kimmerer, 201.
78. Graeber and Wengrow, *Dawn of Everything*, 301–02.
79. Graeber and Wengrow, 45. Cf. Francesca Polletta's *Freedom Is an Endless Meeting* (Chicago: University of Chicago Press, 2004) for more examples of the archetype of politicality.
80. Here's Hannah Arendt in *The Human Condition*: "To live together in the world means essential that a world of things is between those who have it in common, as a table is located between those who sit around it; the world, like every in-between, relates and separates men at the same time"; Arendt, *The Human Condition* (Chicago: University of Chicago Press, 1957), 52.
81. Jane Bennett, *Vibrant Matter* (Durham, NC: Duke University Press, 2009), 83.
82. Bennett, *Vibrant Matter*, 24
83. Bennett, 24. Bennett extends Spinoza's ideas, thinking with Gilles Deleuze and Felix Guattari, by theorizing assemblages as an "event space or style or structuration." Here's Bennett: "Assemblages are ad hoc groupings of diverse elements, of vibrant materials of all sorts. Assemblages are living, throbbing confederations that are able to function despite the persistent presence of energies that confound them from within"; Bennett, *Vibrant Matter*, 23–24.
84. Bennett, *Vibrant Matter*, 29.
85. On the question of distributed agency, see also Martin Crowley, *Accidental Agents: Ecological Politics Beyond the Human* (New York: Columbia University Press, 2022).
86. Cf. Iris Marion Young, *Inclusion and Democracy* (Oxford: Oxford University Press, 2002).
87. Cf. Bonnie Honig, *Public Things: Democracy in Disrepair* (New York: Fordham University Press, 2017); and Michael Sandel, *Democracy's Discontent* (Cambridge, MA: Harvard University Press, 2022).
88. Cf. James Martel, *Subverting the Leviathan* (New York: Columbia University Press, 2007); and Scott, *Art of Not Being Governed*.

89. Hahrie Han and colleagues suggest how community organizations can develop multiform capacities of response along these lines. Hahrie Han, Elizabeth McKenna, and Michelle Oyakawa, *Prisms of the People* (Chicago: University of Chicago Press, 2021).

90. Jürgen Habermas, *Between Facts and Norms*, trans. Willian Rehg (Cambridge, MA: MIT Press, 1998).

91. Max Horkheimer, "Traditional and Critical Theory," in *Critical Theory*, translated by Matthew J. O'Connell (New York: Continuum Press, 2002), 217.

92. Norman O. Brown, *Love's Body* (Berkeley: University of California Press, 1966), 210.

93. Brown, *Love's Body*, 209.

94. Kimmerer, *Braiding Sweetgrass*, 304

95. Grace Lee Boggs et al., "New Questions for an American Revolution," in *Conversations in Maine*, new ed. (Minneapolis: University of Minnesota Press, 2018), 105.

96. Carl Jung, "Mind and Earth," in *The Collected Works of C. G. Jung*, vol. 10 (London: Routledge, 1991), 31.

97. Jung, "Mind and Earth," 31.

98. Jung, 31.

99. Jung, 32.

100. Episcopal Church, *The Book of Common Prayer and Administration of the Sacraments and Other Rites and Ceremonies of the Church: Together with the Psalter or Psalms of David According to the Use of the Episcopal Church* (New York: Seabury Press, 1979).

101. David Abram, *Becoming Animal* (New York: Random House, 2010), 99.

102. "The miracle that saves the world, the realm of human affairs, from its normal, 'natural,' ruin is ultimately the fact of natality, in which the faculty of action is ontologically rooted. It is, in other words, the birth of new men and the new beginning, the action they are capable of by virtue of being born"; Arendt, *Human Condition*, 247.

103. Brown, *Love's Body*, 189.

104. Jung, *Memories, Dreams, Reflections*, 4.

105. Consider Jung on the rhizome: "Life has always seemed to me like a plant that lives on its rhizome. Its true life is invisible, hidden in the rhizome. The part that appears above ground lasts only a single summer. Then it withers away—an ephemeral apparition. When we think of the unending growth and decay of life and civilizations, we cannot escape the

impressions of absolute nullity. Yet I have never lost a sense of something that lives and endures underneath the eternal flux. What we see is the blossom, which passes. The rhizome remains"; Jung, *Memories, Dreams, Reflections*, 4.

106. Cf. Arendt on natality in Arendt, *Human Condition*.

107. See Abdullah Öcalan, *Sociology of Freedom: Manifesto for a Democratic Civilization*, vol. 3 (Binghamton, NY: PM Press, 2020).

108. Alexis Pauline Gumbs, "Preface" to *Undrowned: Black Feminist Lessons from Marine Mammals* (Oakland, CA: AK Press, 2020).

109. "Video: The Commonwealth of Breath" (lecture), Center for the Study of World Religions, Harvard Divinity School, April 9, 2019, https://cswr .hds.harvard.edu/news/2021/05/10/video-commonwealth-breath -climate-and-consciousness-more-human-world.

110. David Abram, "The Commonwealth of Breath" (lecture at the Center for the Study of World Religions, Harvard University Divinity School), April 9. 2019, https://cswr.hds.harvard.edu/news/2021/05/10/video-commonwealth -breath-climate-and-consciousness-more-human-world.

111. Kimmerer, *Braiding Sweetgrass*, ix.

112. Luce Irigaray and Michael Marder, *Through Vegetal Being* (New York: Columbia University Press, 2016), 29.

113. David Abram, *The Spell of the Sensuous* (New York: Vintage, 1996), 230.

114. Abram, *Spell of the Sensuous*, 235.

115. Abram, 236.

116. Luce Irigaray, *The Forgetting of Air in Martin Heidegger* (Austin: University of Texas Press, 1999), 20.

117. Gumbs, *Undrowned*, chap. 2.

118. Cf. Achille Mbembe, "The Universal Right to Breathe," *Critical Inquiry* 47, no. 52 (Winter 2021): 58–62.

119. Norman O. Brown, "A Reply to Herbert Marcuse." *Commentary*, March 1967, 83.

3. DEMOCRATIC RITUALS OF EARTHLY ENTANGLEMENT

The epigraphs from this chapter are from Romand Coles, *Visionary Pragmatism* (Durham, NC: Duke University Press, 2016), 101–102; and Silvia Federici, *Re-Enchanting the World: Feminism and the Politics of the Commons* (New York: PM Press/Kairos, 2018), 8.

1. Cedric Robinson, *Terms of Order: Political Science and the Myth of Leadership* (Chapel Hill: University of North Carolina Press, 2016).

2. Sheldon S. Wolin, *The Presence of the Past: Essays on the State and the Constitution* (Baltimore: John Hopkins University Press, 1989), 180–191.

3. Sheldon S. Wolin, *Democracy, Incorporated: Managed Democracy and the Specter of Inverted Totalitarianism* (Princeton, NJ: Princeton University Press, 2008).

4. See Jeffrey C. Alexander, "Watergate as Democratic Ritual," in *The Meanings of Social Life: A Cultural Sociology* (Oxford: Oxford University Press, 2003), 155–178; Alexander, *Performance and Power* (Hoboken, NJ: Wiley, 2013); and Jeffrey Edward Green, *The Eyes of the People: Democracy in an Age of Spectatorship* (Oxford: Oxford University Press, 2009).

5. Joan Didion, *Political Fictions* (New York: Vintage, 2002).

6. Byung-Chul Han, *The Disappearance of Rituals*, trans. Daniel Steuer (Cambridge: Polity, 2020).

7. Glen Coulthard and Leanne Betasamosake Simpson, "Grounded Normativity/Place-Based Solidarity." *American Quarterly* 68, no. 2 (June 2016): 254.

8. Robert N. Bellah, "The Ritual Roots of Society and Culture," in *Handbook of the Sociology of Religion*, ed. Michelle Dillon (Cambridge: Cambridge University Press, 2003), 32.

9. Jeffrey C. Alexander and Phillip Smith, "Introduction" to *The Cambridge Companion to Durkheim*, ed. Alexander and Smith (Cambridge: Cambridge University Press, 2005), 13.

10. Robin Wall Kimmerer, *Braiding Sweetgrass* (Minneapolis: Milkweed Editions, 2015), 249.

11. Mircea Eliade, *The Sacred and the Profane*, trans. Willard R. Trask (New York: Harcourt Brace Janovich, 1987), 79.

12. Joseph Campbell, *Masks of God: Creative Mythology* (New York: Penguin, 1995), 3.

13. Charles Taylor, *The Ethics of Authenticity* (Cambridge, MA: Harvard University Press, 1992).

14. Han, *Disappearance of Ritual*, 3.

15. Han, 11.

16. Campbell, *Masks of God*, 37.

17. Molly Farneth, *The Politics of Ritual* (Princeton, NJ: Princeton University Press, 2023), 11–12.

18. Farneth, *Politics of Ritual*, 13.

19. Rupert Sheldrake, *The Presence of the Past: Morphic Resonance and the Memory of Nature* (Toronto: Park Street Press, 2012), 301.
20. Sheldrake, *Presence of the Past*, 307.
21. David Graeber and David Wengrow, *The Dawn of Everything* (New York: Farrar, Strauss, and Giroux, 2021), 117.
22. Graeber and Wengrow, *Dawn of Everything*, 545n54.
23. As Thomas Thornton writes, ritual is "emplacement"; Thornton, *Being and Place Among the Tlingit* (Seattle: University of Washington Press, 2008), 175. Paulina Ochoa Espejo's conception of "place-based practices" also speaks to this by explicitly developing ideas of membership and community around place. In *On Borders*, she locates these in watersheds that convene human and nonhuman actors; Ochoa Espejo, *On Borders: Territories, Legitimacy, and the Rights of Place* (Oxford: Oxford University Press, 2020). Recently she's written on *pueblos* as places that bring together Indigenous and non-Indigenous populations; Ochoa Espejo, "Territorial Rights for Individuals, States, or Pueblos? Answers from Indigenous Land Struggles in Colonial Spanish America," *Perspectives on Politics* 21, no. 1 (2022): 94–108.
24. Leanne Betasamosake Simpson, *As We Have Always Done* (Minneapolis: University of Minnesota Press, 2021), 17.
25. For a review of the Idle No More protests, see Ali Aslam, *Ordinary Democracy: Sovereignty and Citizenship Beyond the Neoliberal Impasse* (Oxford: Oxford University Press, 2016).
26. Simpson, *As We Have Always Done*, 224.
27. Simpson argues for the need to rethink processes by which we live. Social movement theory is inadequate, because it focuses on strategic goals vs. expressive politics, i.e., forms of life: *Dancing on Our Turtle's Back* (Winnipeg: Arbeiter Ring, 2011), 16–17.
28. Simpson, *As We Have Always Done*, 2.
29. Simpson, 8.
30. Simpson, 20.
31. Simpson, 23.
32. Simpson, 23. See Simpson's description of the clan system as "emergent," appearing when needed and giving people a stake in decisions through participatory processes.
33. Simpson, 153.
34. Simpson, 159 and 173.
35. Simpson, 24; Simpson, *Dancing on Our Turtle's Back*, 66.

36. Simpson, *Dancing on Our Turtle's Back*, 91; quoting Sákéj Youngblood Henderson, *First Nations Jurisprudence and Aboriginal Rights* (Saskatoon: Native Law Centre, University of Saskatchewan, 2006), 153.

37. Another example is Simpson's spotlighting of Kwe, the fluid gender norms of the Nishnaabeg. Kwe does not adhere to rigid gender stereotypes (29). Kwe offers a "resurgent method" (27). See Simpson, *As We Have Always Done*.

38. Simpson, *As We Have Always Done*, 2. On Indigenous refusal, see also Glen Sean Coulthard, *Red Skin, White Masks: Rejecting the Colonial Politics of Recognition* (Minneapolis: University of Minnesota Press, 2014); and Audra Simpson, *Mohawk Interruptus: Political Life Across the Borders of the Settler States* (Durham, NC: Duke University Press, 2014). On refusal in other contexts, see recent work by Bonnie Honig, *A Feminist Theory of Refusal* (Cambridge: Harvard University Press, 2021), and Saidiya Hartman, *Wayward Lives, Beautiful Experiments* (New York: Norton, 2019).

39. Simpson, *As We Have Always Done*, 17; Neil Roberts, *Freedom as Marronage* (Chicago: University of Chicago Press, 2015), 4–5.

40. Simpson, *As We Have Always Done*, 196.

41. Gerald Vizenor, *Manifest Manners: Narratives on Postindian Survivance* (Lincoln: University of Nebraska Press, 1999).

42. Simpson, *As We Have Always Done*, 196.

43. Simpson, 196.

44. Simpson, 17.

45. Simpson, 196.

46. Simpson, 18.

47. Simpson, 30.

48. Glen Coulthard and Leanne Betasamosake Simpson, "Grounded Normativity/Place-Based Solidarity," *American Quarterly* 68, no. 2 (June 2016): 254.

49. Simpson, *As We Have Always Done*, 155. Emphasis in the original.

50. Simpson, 154.

51. Simpson, 29.

52. Simpson, 8.

53. See Simpson, *Dancing on Our Turtle's Back*: on elders of Long Lake learning freedom from eagles (18); on the agency of maple trees (107); and on eels taught Nishnabaag migration (88). See Simpson, *As We Have Always Been*, on the Hoof Clan's refusal and flight (58–61).

54. Simpson, *Dancing on Our Turtle's Back*, 88

55. Simpson, *Dancing on Our Turtle's Back*, 88. Simpson's story of the discovery of maple syrup, in which a child discovers this practice by observing a squirrel, offers another example. She tells this in three different ways in Leanne Betasamosake Simpson, *The Gift Is in the Making* (Winnipeg: Portage and Main Press, 2013); Simpson, Nishnaabeg Intelligence and Rebellious Transformation," *Decolonization: Indigeneity, Education and Society* 3, no. 3 (2014): 1–25; and Simpson, *As We Have Always Done.*

56. Simpson, *As We Have Always Done*, 165.

57. Simpson, 6.

58. Cf. Simpson here: "Theory within this context is generated from the ground up, and its power stems from its living resonance within individuals and collectives"; Simpson, *As We Have Always Done*, 151.

59. Kali Akuno and Ajamu Nangwaya, eds., *Jackson Rising* (Wakefield: Daraja Press, 2017), 3.

60. We rely here primarily on recent books compiling writings about Cooperation Jackson, which include both programmatic materials and journalism about the varied programs: Akuno and Nangwaya, *Jackson Rising*; and Kali Akuno and Matt Meyer, eds., *Jackson Rising Redux: Lessons on Building the Future in the Present* (Oakland, CA: PM Press, 2023).

61. Akuno and Nangwaya, *Jackson Rising*, 88–89.

62. Akuno and Nangwaya, 91.

63. Akuno and Nangwaya, 95.

64. Bioneers, "How Jackson, Mississippi, Imagines a Cooperative Future," https://bioneers.org/jackson-mississippi-imagines-a-cooperative-future-zmbz2007/ (accessed May 20, 2023).

65. This forms a "self reinforcing chain wherein Freedom Farms produces food that is sold and consumed at Nubia's Place Cafe, the waste from which nourishes the crops produced by Freedom Farms"; Akuno and Nangwaya, *Jackson Rising*, 20.

66. Vijay Phulwani, "A Splendid Failure? Black Reconstruction and Du Bois's Tragic Vision of Politics," in *A Political Companion to W. E. B. DuBois*, ed. Nicholas Bromell (Lexington: University of Kentucky Press, 2018), 271–302.

67. Akuno and Nangwaya, *Jackson Rising*, 90.

68. Cf. Charles M. Payne, *I've Got the Light of Freedom: The Organizing Tradition and the Mississippi Freedom Struggle* (Berkeley: University of California Press, 2007).

69. Akuno and Nangwaya, *Jackson Rising*, 5.

70. Akuno and Nangwaya, 5

71. Cf. George Ciccariello-Maher, *Building the Commune* (New York: Verso, 2016).

72. Akuno and Nangwaya, *Jackson Rising*, 8.

73. Akuno and Nangwaya, 167.

74. Justice 4 Jackson, "Help Us Fix Jackson's Water System and Build More Autonomy and People Power in the City," Cooperation Jackson, September 5, 2022, https://cooperationjackson.org/announcementsblog /justice4jackson.

75. Cf. Edward Onaci, *Free the Land: The Republic of New Afrika and the Pursuit of a Black Nation-State* (Chapel Hill: University of North Carolina Press, 2020).

76. J. T. Roane, *Dark Agoras: Insurgent Black Social Life and the Politics of Place* (New York: New York University Press, 2023), 32.

77. Akuno and Nangwaya, *Jackson Rising*, xii.

78. Akuno and Nangwaya, xii.

79. Bioneers, "How Jackson, Mississippi, Imagines."

80. Mark R. Warren, *Dry Bones Rattling: Community Building to Revitalize American Democracy* (Princeton, NJ: Princeton University Press, 2001), 42–43.

81. Warren, *Dry Bones Rattling*, 47.

82. Romand Coles gives examples of one-on-one questions in his article "Moving Democracy:" "Typically, IAF leaders and activists will begin such meetings with questions designed to encourage the other to begin probing the visceral depths of their public perceptions and involvements: What is it about your basic sense of things that really propelled you to become a [social worker, pastor, imam, teacher, union member, etc.]? What contribution in your work as county commissioner, or your involvement in this community, do you most dream of being remembered for? There is a lot of suffering in this neighborhood, what are the things that most anger you about how this city is run? Being a pastor, what do you think Jesus and the Beloved Community mean for Durham, N.C.?" Coles, "Moving Democracy: Industrial Areas Foundation Social Movements and the Political Arts of Listening, Traveling, and Tabling," *Political Theory* 32, no. 5 (2004): 685.

83. Jeffrey Stout, *Blessed Are the Organized: Grassroots Democracy in America* (Princeton, NJ: Princeton University Press, 2010), 45.

84. Stout, *Blessed Are the Organized*, 45.
85. Saul D. Alinsky, *Reveille for Radicals* (New York: Vintage, 1987), 99.
86. Alinsky, *Reveille for Radicals*, 100.
87. Alinsky, 172.
88. Stout, *Blessed Are the Organized*, 130.
89. Stout, 95.
90. Marco Iacoboni, *Mirroring People: The Science of How We Connect with Others* (New York: Farrar, Straus and Giroux, 2008), 152 and 55; quoted in Romand Coles, *Visionary Pragmatism* (Durham, NC: Duke University Press, 2016), 42.
91. Sarah Blaffer Hrdy, *Mothers and Others* (Cambridge, MA: Harvard University Press, 2009).
92. Coles, *Visionary Pragmatism*, 41.
93. Coles, 188.
94. Coles, 51.
95. Coles, 105.
96. Coles, 65.
97. Stout, *Blessed Are the Organized*, 37–38.
98. Coles, *Visionary Pragmatism*, 58.
99. As Coles notes, though he focuses on food, "it would be easy to extend such an analysis to other mega-circulations such as energy, finance, water, pharmaceuticals, vehicles, and weapons"; Coles, *Visionary Pragmatism*, 79.
100. Coles, *Visionary Pragmatism*, 96. We would note that Salatin's story is more complicated than this mention suggests, given both his record of nativist, racist remarks as well as the broader settler colonial basis of neo-republican back-to-the-land homesteading. See Tom Philpott, "Joel Salatin's Unsustainable Myth," *Mother Jones*, November 19, 2020, https://www.motherjones.com/food/2020/11/joel-salatin-chris-newman-farming-rotational-grazing-agriculture/.
101. Coles, *Visionary Pragmatism*, 98.
102. Cf. Danielle Hanley on choral politics: Hanley, "Choreographing Affective Solidarity: The Choral Politics of Responding to Loss," *Theory and Event* 25, no. 4 (October 2022): 873–899.
103. Gloria E. Anzaldúa, *A Light in the Dark/Luz en lo Oscuro* (Durham, NC: Duke University Press, 2015).
104. Alexis Pauline Gumbs, *Undrowned: Black Feminist Lessons from Marine Mammals* (Oakland, CA: AK Press, 2020).

105. Lawrence Goodwyn, *The Populist Moment: A Short History of Agrarian Revolt in America* (New York: Oxford University Press, 1978). See also Laura Grattan, *Populism's Power: Radical Grassroots Democracy in America* (Oxford: Oxford University Press, 2018).

106. Nathan Schneider, *Everything for Everyone: The Radical Tradition That Is Shaping the Next Economy* (New York: Nation Books, 2018); John Curl, *For All the People: Uncovering the Hidden History of Cooperation, Cooperative Movements, and Communalism in America* (Oakland: PM Press, 2012).

107. Gar Alperovitz, *What Then Must We Do? Straight Talk About the Next American Revolution* (White River Junction, VT: Chelsea Green, 2013).

108. Fred Moten's language of "Black sociality" corresponds to sociality as a democratic archetype as well. And then there's this gem in Moten's conversation with Stefano Harney and Stevphen Shukaitis: "Because I figure that performances of a certain mode of sociality also already imply the ongoing production of the theory of sociality. I mean, I'm into that, just like I'm into horny old Socrates when he sees some beautiful young boys he just wants to get next to, and they say, 'man, come to the palestra because we need to talk about friendship,' and he's like, 'oh yeah, I'll come'"; Stefano Harney and Fred Moten, *Undercommons: Fugitive Planning and Black Study* (New York: Minor Compositions, 2013), 158. Now that's sociality!

109. J. K. Gibson-Graham, *A Post-Capitalist Politics* (Minneapolis: University of Minnesota Press, 2006).

110. Ciccariello-Maher, *Building the Commune.*

111. Ercan Aygoga, "The Concept of Democratic Confederalism and How it is Implemented in Rojava/Kurdistan," in Akuno and Meyer, *Jackson Redux*, 383–399.

112. Deborah Bird Rose, *Reports from a Wild Country* (Randwick: University of New South Wales Press, 2004); and Rose, *Shimmer: Flying Fox Exuberance in Worlds of Peril* (Edinburgh: University of Edinburgh Press, 2022). See further work on multispecies ethnography as articulated by Eben Kirksey and Stefan Helmreich, "The Emergence of Multispecies Ethnography," *Cultural Anthropology* 25, no. 4 (2010): 545–576.

113. Anna Lowenhaupt Tsing, "The Sociality of Birds," in *Kin: Thinking with Deborah Bird Rose*, ed. Thom van Dooren and Matthew Chrulew (Durham, NC: Duke University Press, 2022), 15–32.

114. Merlin Sheldrake, *Entangled Life: How Fungi Make Our Worlds, Change Our Minds, and Change Our Futures* (New York: Random House, 2021), 211–212.

115. Sheldrake, *Entangled Life*, 213.

116. Recent successes in BBO have also pushed toward more ecologically entangled achievements, such as New York State Energy Research and Development Authority (NYSERDA) and Metro IAF's recent securing of $4 million to assist religious congregations in creating and implementing a decarbonization plan for their buildings. See New York State, "NYSERDA and Metro IAF Announce $4 Million Award to Assist Religious Congregations in Creating and Implementing a Decarbonization Plan for Their Buildings," April 22, 2021, https://www.nyserda.ny.gov /About/Newsroom/2021-Announcements/2021-04-22-NYSERDA-and -Metro-IAF-Announce-4-Million-Award-to-Assist-Religious -Congregations-in-Creating-and-Implementing-a-Decarbonization -Plan-for-Their-Buildings.

117. We would also point to theoretical efforts to conceptualize "parliaments of things" or "parliaments of worms" by Jane Bennett and Bruno Latour as reflections on these emerging examples of the democratic archetype of politicality.

118. Occidental Arts and Ecology Center, "Permaculture for the People," https://oaec.org/projects/liberation-permaculture/.

119. Deva R. Woodly, *Reckoning: Black Lives Matter and the Democratic Necessity of Social Movements* (New York: Oxford University Press, 2021).

120. Charlene Carruthers, *Unapologetic: A Queer, Black, Feminist Mandate for Radical Movements* (Boston: Beacon Press, 2018).

121. Paul Apostolidis, *Breaks in the Chain: What Immigrant Workers Can Teach America About Democracy* (Minneapolis: University of Minnesota Press, 2010).

122. Harney and Moten, *Undercommons*, 18.

123. Lia Haro and Romand Coles, "Reimagining Fugitive Democracy and Transformative Sanctuary with Black Frontline Communities in the Underground Railroad." *Political Theory*, 47, no. 5 (2019): 646–673.

124. Pennelys Droz, "The Healing Work of Returning Stolen Lands," *Yes! Magazine*, November 15, 2021, https://www.yesmagazine.org/issue/a-new -social-justice/2021/11/15/return-stolen-lands-wiyot-tribe.

125. On emergence as a strategy (pursued in part through attunement), see Adrienne Maree Brown, *Emergent Strategy: Shaping Change, Changing Worlds* (Chico, CA: AK Press, 2017).

126. Hahrie Han, Elizabeth McKenna, and Michelle Oyakawa, *Prisms of the People* (Chicago: University of Chicago Press, 2021), 22.

BIBLIOGRAPHY

Abram, David. *Becoming Animal.* New York: Random House, 2010.
——. *The Spell of the Sensuous.* New York: Vintage, 1996.
——. "Video: The Commonwealth of Breath" (lecture). Center for the Study
   of World Religions, Harvard Divinity School. April 9, 2019. https://cswr
   .hds.harvard.edu/news/2021/05/10/video-commonwealth-breath-climate
   -and-consciousness-more-human-world.
Akuno, Kali, and Matt Meyer, eds. *Jackson Rising Redux: Lessons on Building
   the Future in the Present.* Oakland, CA: PM Press, 2023.
Akuno, Kali, and Ajamu Nangwaya, eds. *Jackson Rising.* Wakefield: Daraja
   Press, 2017.
Alexander, Jeffrey C. *Performance and Power.* London: Polity Press, 2013.
——. "Watergate as Democratic Ritual." In *The Meanings of Social Life: A
   Cultural Sociology,* 155–178. Oxford: Oxford University Press, 2003.
Alexander, Jeffrey C., and Phillip Smith, eds. *The Cambridge Companion to
   Durkheim.* Cambridge: Cambridge University Press, 2005.
Alinsky, Saul D. *Reveille for Radicals.* New York: Vintage, 1987.
Allen, Amy. *Critique on the Couch: Why Critical Theory Needs Psychoanalysis.*
   New York: Columbia University Press, 2020.
Alperovitz, Gar. *What Then Must We Do? Straight Talk About the Next Amer-
   ican Revolution.* White River Junction, VT: Chelsea Green, 2013.

Anker, Elisabeth R. *ugly freedoms*. Durham, NC: Duke University Press, 2022.

Anzaldúa, Gloria E. *A Light in the Dark/Luz en lo Oscuro*. Durham, NC: Duke University Press, 2015.

Apostolidis, Paul. *Breaks in the Chain: What Immigrant Workers Can Teach America About Democracy*. Minneapolis: University of Minnesota Press, 2010.

Arendt, Hannah. *The Human Condition*. Chicago: University of Chicago Press, 1957.

Aslam, Ali. *Ordinary Democracy: Sovereignty and Citizenship Beyond the Neoliberal Impasse*. Oxford: Oxford University Press, 2016.

Aslam, Ali, David McIvor, and Joel Schlosser. "Critical Exchange: Visionary Political Theory." *Contemporary Political Theory*. DOI: 10.1057/s41296-023-00627-3.

——. "Democracy and the Unconscious." *Polity* 56, no. 1 (January 2024): 40–64.

——. "Democratic Theory When Democracy Is Fugitive." *Democratic Theory* 6, no. 2 (Winter 2019): 27–40.

Bellah, Robert N. "The Ritual Roots of Society and Culture." In *Handbook of the Sociology of Religion*, ed. Michelle Dillon, 31–44. Cambridge: Cambridge University Press, 2003.

Beltrán, Cristina. *Cruelty as Citizenship*. Minneapolis: University of Minnesota Press, 2020.

Benjamin, Walter. "The Image of Proust." In *Illuminations*, trans. H. Zohn, 201–216. New York: Schocken Books, 1968.

Bennett, Jane. *Vibrant Matter*. Durham, NC: Duke University Press, 2009.

Berardi, Franco. *The Third Unconscious*. London: Verso, 2021.

Bioneers. "How Jackson, Mississippi, Imagines a Cooperative Future." Accessed May 20, 2023. https://bioneers.org/jackson-mississippi-imagines-a-cooperative-future-zmbz2007/.

Blok, Josine H. "Gentrifying Genealogy: On the Genesis of the Athenian Autochthony Myth." In *Antike Mythen: Medien, Transformationen, und Konstruckionen*, ed. Ueli Dill and Christine Wilde, 251–275. Berlin: De Gruyter, 2009.

Bly, Robert. *Iron John: A Book About Men*. Cambridge, MA: Da Capo Press, 2013.

——. *A Little Book on the Human Shadow*. New York: HarperCollins, 1998.

Boggs, Grace Lee, Jimmy Boggs, Freddy Paine, and Lyman Paine. *Conversations in Maine*. New ed. Minneapolis: University of Minnesota Press, 2018.

Bookchin, Murray. *The Ecology of Freedom*. Chico, CA: AK Press, 1982.

Breaugh, Martin. *The Plebeian Experience*. New York: Columbia University Press, 2007.

Brennan, Jason. *Against Democracy*. Princeton, NJ: Princeton University Press, 2017.

Brown, Adrienne Maree. *Emergent Strategy: Shaping Change, Changing Worlds*. Chico, CA: AK Press, 2017.

Brown, Norman O. *Love's Body*. Berkeley: University of California Press, 1966.

——. "A Reply to Herbert Marcuse." *Commentary*, March 1967, 83–84.

Bruyneel, Kevin. *Settler Memory: The Disavowal of Indigeneity and the Politics of Race in the United States*. Chapel Hill: University of North Carolina Press, 2021.

Cadena, Marisol de la. *Earth Beings: Ecologies of Practice Across Andean Worlds*. Durham, NC: Duke University Press, 2015.

Campbell, Joseph. *Masks of God: Creative Mythology*. New York: Penguin, 1995.

Carruthers, Charlene. *Unapologetic: A Queer, Black, Feminist Mandate for Radical Movements*. Boston: Beacon Press, 2018.

Ciccariello-Maher, George. *Building the Commune*. New York: Verso, 2016.

Coles, Romand. "Moving Democracy: Industrial Areas Foundation Social Movements and the Political Arts of Listening, Traveling, and Tabling." *Political Theory* 32, no. 5 (2004): 678–705.

——. *Visionary Pragmatism*. Durham, NC: Duke University Press, 2016.

Connolly, William E. *Capitalism and Christianity, American Style*. Durham, NC: Duke University Press, 2008.

——. *Climate Machines, Fascist Drives, and Truth*. Durham, NC: Duke University Press, 2019.

——. *Facing the Planetary: Entangled Humanism and the Politics of Swarming*. Durham, NC: Duke University Press, 2017.

——. *The Fragility of Things*. Durham, NC: Duke University Press, 2013.

Coulthard, Glen Sean. *Red Skin, White Masks: Rejecting the Colonial Politics of Recognition*. Minneapolis: University of Minnesota Press, 2014.

Coulthard, Glen, and Leanne Betasamosake Simpson. "Grounded Norma-
tivity/Place-Based Solidarity." *American Quarterly* 68, no. 2 (June 2016):
249–255.

Crowley, Martin. *Accidental Agents: Ecological Politics Beyond the Human.* New
York: Columbia University Press, 2022

Curl, John. *For All the People: Uncovering the Hidden History of Cooperation,
Cooperative Movements, and Communalism in America.* Oakland: PM
Press, 2012.

Deloria, Vine, Jr., and Daniel Wildcat. *Power and Place: Indian Education in
America.* Golden, CO: Fulcrum Resources, 2001.

Descola, Philippe. *Beyond Nature and Culture.* Trans. J. Lloyd. Chicago: University of Chicago Press, 2013.

——. *The Ecology of Others.* Trans. G. Godbout and B. Luley. Chicago:
Prickly Paradigm Press, 2013.

Didion, Joan. *Political Fictions.* New York: Vintage, 2002.

Droz, Pennelys. "The Healing Work of Returning Stolen Lands." *Yes! Magazine.* November 15, 2021. https://www.yesmagazine.org/issue/a-new
-social-justice/2021/11/15/return-stolen-lands-wiyot-tribe.

Dryzek, John. *The Politics of the Earth.* Oxford: Oxford University Press, 1997.

Eliade, Mircea. *The Sacred and the Profane.* Trans. Willard R. Trask. New
York: Harcourt Brace Janovich, 1987.

Episcopal Church. *The Book of Common Prayer and Administration of the Sacraments and Other Rites and Ceremonies of the Church: Together with the Psalter or Psalms of David According to the Use of the Episcopal Church.* New
York: Seabury Press, 1979.

Escobar, Arturo. *Pluriversal Politics: The Real and the Possible.* Durham, NC:
Duke University Press, 2020.

Farneth, Molly. *The Politics of Ritual.* Princeton, NJ: Princeton University
Press, 2023.

Federici, Silvia. *Re-enchanting the World: Feminism and the Politics of the Commons.* New York: PM Press/Kairos, 2018.

Foucault, Michel. *Security, Territory, Population.* Trans. Graham Burchell.
New York: Palgrave, 2009.

Frank, Jill. "Athenian Democracy and Its Critics." *Ethnic and Racial Studies*
42, no. 8 (2019): 1306–1312.

Freud, Sigmund. *The Interpretation of Dreams.* London: Penguin, 1983.

——. *Totem and Taboo.* London: Routledge, 2015.

Fujikane, Candace. *Mapping Abundance for a Planetary Future*. Durham, NC: Duke University Press, 2021.

Gaventa, John. *Power and Powerlessness: Quiescence and Rebellion in an Appalachian Valley*. Champagne: University of Illinois Press, 1982.

Gordon, Avery. *Ghostly Matters: Haunting and the Sociological Imagination*. New ed. Minneapolis: University of Minnesota Press, 2008. First published in 1997.

Graeber, David. "There Never Was a West." In *Possibilities: Essays on Hierarchy, Rebellion, Desire*, 329–374. Oakland, CA: AK Press, 2007.

Graeber, David, and David Wengrow. *The Dawn of Everything*. New York: Farrar, Strauss and Giroux, 2021.

Grattan, Laura. *Populism's Power: Radical Grassroots Democracy in America*. Oxford: Oxford University Press, 2018.

Green, Jeffrey Edward. *The Eyes of the People: Democracy in an Age of Spectatorship*. Oxford: Oxford University Press, 2009.

Gibson-Graham, J. K. "Beyond Global vs. Local: Economic Politics Outside the Binary Frame." In *Geographies of Power: Placing Scale*, ed. Andrew Herod and Melissa W. Wright, 25–60. Malden, MA: Blackwell, 2002.

——. *A Post-Capitalist Politics*. Minneapolis: University of Minnesota Press, 2006.

Goodwyn, Lawrence. *The Populist Moment: A Short History of Agrarian Revolt in America*. New York: Oxford University Press, 1978.

Guattari, Felix. *The Guattari Reader*. Ed. Gary Genosko. Cambridge, MA: Blackwell, 1996.

——. *The Three Ecologies*. London: Athlone Press, 2000.

Gumbs, Alexis Pauline. *Undrowned: Black Feminist Lessons from Marine Mammals*. Oakland, CA: AK Press, 2020.

Gurwitsch, Alexander G. "Über den Begriff des embryonalen Feldes." *Archiv für Entwicklungsmechanik der Organismen* 51 (1922): 388–415.

Habermas, Jürgen. *Between Facts and Norms*. Trans. Willian Rehg. Cambridge, MA: MIT Press, 1998.

Han, Byung-Chul. *The Disappearance of Rituals*. Trans. Daniel Steuer. Cambridge: Polity, 2020.

Han, Hahrie, Elizabeth McKenna, and Michelle Oyakawa. *Prisms of the People*. Chicago: University of Chicago Press, 2021.

Hanchard, Michael. *The Spectre of Race: How Discrimination Haunts Western Democracy*. Princeton, NJ: Princeton University Press, 2018.

Hanley, Danielle. "Choreographing Affective Solidarity: The Choral Politics of Responding to Loss." *Theory and Event* 25, no. 4 (October 2022): 873–899.

Haraway, Donna. *Staying with the Trouble*. Durham, NC: Duke University Press, 2016.

Harney, Stefano, and Fred Moten. *Undercommons: Fugitive Planning and Black Study*. New York: Minor Compositions, 2013.

Haro, Lia, and Romand Coles. "Reimagining Fugitive Democracy and Transformative Sanctuary with Black Frontline Communities in the Underground Railroad." *Political Theory*, 47, no. 5 (2019): 646–673.

Hartman, Saidiya. *Wayward Lives, Beautiful Experiments*. New York: Norton, 2019.

Henderson, Sákéj Youngblood. *First Nations Jurisprudence and Aboriginal Rights*. Saskatoon: Native Law Centre, University of Saskatchewan, 2006.

Hernandez, Jessica. *Fresh Banana Leaves: Healing Indigenous Landscapes Through Indigenous Science*. New York: Penguin Random House, 2022.

Honig, Bonnie. *A Feminist Theory of Refusal*. Cambridge, MA: Harvard University Press, 2021.

——. *Public Things: Democracy in Disrepair*. New York: Fordham University Press, 2017.

Horkheimer, Max. "Traditional and Critical Theory." In *Critical Theory*, trans. Matthew J. O'Connell, 188–243. New York: Continuum Press, 2002.

Horkheimer, Max, and Theodor Adorno. *Dialectic of Enlightenment: Philosophical Fragments*. Trans. Edward Jephcott. Palo Alto, CA: Stanford University Press, 2002.

Hrdy, Sarah Blaffer. *Mothers and Others*. Cambridge, MA: Harvard University Press, 2009.

Iacoboni, Marco. *Mirroring People: The Science of How We Connect with Others*. New York: Farrar, Straus and Giroux, 2008.

Ignatov, Anatoli. "African Orature as Ecophilosophy: Tuning In to the Voices of the Land." *Geohumanities* 2, no. 1 (2016): 76–91.

——. "The Earth as a Gift-Giving Ancestor: Nietzsche's Perspectivism and African Animism." *Political Theory* 45, no. 1 (February 2017): 52–75.

——. "Practices of Eco-sensation: Opening Doors of Perception to the Nonhuman." *Theory and Event* 14, no. 2 (2011). https://doi.org/10.1353/tae.2011 .0016.

Irigaray, Luce. *The Forgetting of Air in Martin Heidegger*. Austin: University of Texas Press, 1999.

Irigaray, Luce, and Michael Marder. *Through Vegetal Being*. New York: Columbia University Press, 2016.

Irwin, Elizabeth "The Nothoi Come of Age? Illegitimate Sons and Political Unrest in Late Fifth-Century Athens." In *Minderheiten und Migration in der griechisch-römischen Welt: Politische, rechtliche, religiöse und kulturelle Aspekte*, ed. P. Sänger, 75–112. Paderborn, Germany: Schöningh Wissenschaftsverlag.

Isaac, Benjamin. *The Invention of Racism in Classical Antiquity*. Princeton, NJ: Princeton University Press, 2004.

James, C.L.R. "Every Cook Can Govern. A Study of Democracy in Ancient Greece, Its Meaning for Today." *Correspondence* 2, no. 12 (June 1956): 1–20.

Jung, C. G. "Archetypes of the Collective Unconscious." In *The Collected Works of C.G. Jung*, vol. 9, pt. 1, 3–41. Princeton, NJ: Princeton University Press, 1969.

——. *Memories, Dreams, Reflections*. London: Vintage, 1989.

——. "Mind and Earth." In *The Collected Works of C.G. Jung*, vol. 10, 29–49. Princeton, NJ: Princeton University Press, 1969.

——. *The Portable Jung*. New York: Penguin, 1976.

Justice 4 Jackson. "Help Us Fix Jackson's Water System and Build More Autonomy and People Power in the City." Cooperation Jackson, September 5, 2022, https://cooperationjackson.org/announcementsblog /justice4jackson.

Kasimis, Demetra. *The Perpetual Immigrant and the Limits of Athenian Democracy*. Cambridge: Cambridge University Press, 2018.

Krawec, Patty. *Becoming Kin: An Indigenous Call to Unforgetting the Past and Reimagining Our Future*. Minneapolis: Broadleaf Books, 2022.

Kelley, Robin D. G. *Freedom Dreams*. New York: Penguin, 2002.

Kimmerer, Robin Wall. *Braiding Sweetgrass*. Minneapolis: Milkweed Editions, 2015.

Kirksey, Eben. *Emergent Ecologies*. Durham, NC: Duke University Press, 2015.

——. *Freedom in Entangled Worlds: West Papua and the Architecture of Global Power*. Durham, NC: Duke University Press, 2012.

Kirksey, Eben, and Stefan Helmreich. "The Emergence of Multispecies Ethnography." *Cultural Anthropology* 25, no. 4 (2010): 545–576.

Kohn, Eduardo. *How Forests Think: Toward an Anthropology Beyond the Human*. Berkeley: University of California Press, 2013.

Kolbert, Elizabeth. *The Sixth Extinction: An Unnatural History*. New York: Henry Holt, 2014.

Krause, Sharon. *Eco-Emancipation*. Princeton, NJ: Princeton University Press, 2023.

———. "Politics Beyond Persons: Political Theory and the Non-human." *Political Theory* (2016). https://doi.org/10.1177/0090591716651516.

Krenak, Ailton. *Ideas to Postpone the End of the World*. Trans. Anthony Doyle. Toronto: Anansi International, 2020.

Larsen, Soren C., and Jay T. Johnson. *Being Together in Place: Indigenous Coexistence in a More Than Human World*. Minneapolis: University of Minnesota Press, 2017.

Latour, Bruno. *Down to Earth: Politics in the New Climate Regime*. Trans. Catherine Porter. Medford, MA: Polity, 2018.

———. *Facing Gaia: Eight Lectures on the New Climatic Regime*. Trans. Catherine Porter. Medford, MA: Polity, 2017.

Lewis, Sophie. "Cthulhu Plays No Role for Me." *Viewpoint Magazine*. May 8, 2017. https://viewpointmag.com/2017/05/08/cthulhu-plays-no-role-for-me/.

Liboiron, Max. *Pollution Is Colonialism*. Durham, NC: Duke University Press, 2021.

Loraux, Nicole. *The Children of Athena: Athenian Ideas of Citizenship and the Division between the Sexes*. Trans. Caroline Levine. Princeton, NJ: Princeton University Press, 1981.

Malm, Andreas. *How to Blow Up a Pipeline*. New York: Verso, 2020.

Mann, Geoff, and Joel Wainwright. *Climate Leviathan*. New York: Verso, 2020.

Margulies, Jared. "Political Ecology of Desire: Between Extinction, Anxiety, and Flourishing," *Environmental Humanities* 14, no. 2 (2022): 241–264.

Martel, James. *Subverting the Leviathan*. New York: Columbia University Press, 2007.

Mbembe, Achille. "The Universal Right to Breathe," *Critical Inquiry* 47, no. 52 (Winter 2021): S58–S62.

McAfee, Noelle. *Fear of Breakdown: Politics and Psychoanalysis*. New York: Columbia University Press, 2019.

McIvor, David. "The Conscience of a Fugitive." *New Political Science* 38, no. 3 (2016): 411–427.

———. *Mourning in America: Race and the Politics of Loss*. Ithaca, NY: Cornell University Press, 2016.

Meyers, Todd, and Camille Robcis. "Jean Oury and Clinique de La Borde: A Conversation with Camille Robcis." *Somatosphere*, June 3, 2014,

http://somatosphere.net/2014/jean-oury-and-clinique-de-la-borde-a
-conversation-with-camille-robcis.html.

Mignolo, Walter D. *The Politics of Decolonial Investigations*. Durham, NC:
Duke University Press, 2021.

Mills, Charles. *The Racial Contract*. Ithaca, NY: Cornell University Press,
1997.

Mitchell, Timothy. *Carbon Democracy*. New York: Verso, 2013.

Morton, Timothy. *Being Ecological*. Cambridge, MA: MIT Press, 2018.

———. *Humankind: Solidarity with Nonhuman People*. London: Verso, 2017.

New York State. "NYSERDA and Metro IAF Announce $4 Million Award
to Assist Religious Congregations in Creating and Implementing a
Decarbonization Plan for Their Buildings." April 22, 2021. https://www
.nyserda.ny.gov/About/Newsroom/2021-Announcements/2021-04-22
-NYSERDA-and-Metro-IAF-Announce-4-Million-Award-to-Assist
-Religious-Congregations-in-Creating-and-Implementing-a
-Decarbonization-Plan-for-Their-Buildings.

Noble, Brian. "Treaty Ecologies: With Persons, People, Animals, and the
Land." In *Resurgence and Reconciliation: Indigenous-Settler Relations and
Earth Teachings*, ed. Michael Asch, John Borrows, and James Tully, 315–
342. Toronto: University of Toronto Press, 2018.

Norton, Anne. *Wild Democracy*. Oxford: Oxford University Press, 2023.

Ober, Josiah. *Athenian Legacies: Essays on the Politics of Going on Together*.
Princeton, NJ: Princeton University Press, 2005.

———. "On the Original Meaning of Democracy." *Constellations* 15, no. 1
(2008): 3–9.

Öcalan, Abdullah. *Sociology of Freedom: Manifesto for a Democratic Civilization*. Vol. 3. Binghamton, NY: PM Press, 2020.

Occidental Arts and Ecology Center. "Permaculture for the People." https://
oaec.org/projects/liberation-permaculture/.

Ochoa Espejo, Paulina. *On Borders: Territories, Legitimacy, and the Rights of
Place*. Oxford: Oxford University Press, 2020.

———. "Territorial Rights for Individuals, States, or Pueblos? Answers from
Indigenous Land Struggles in Colonial Spanish America." *Perspectives on
Politics* 21, no. 1 (2022): 94–108.

Onaci, Edward. *Free the Land: The Republic of New Afrika and the Pursuit of
a Black Nation-State*. Chapel Hill: University of North Carolina Press,
2020.

Ophuls, William. *Plato's Revenge*. Cambridge, MA: MIT Press, 2011.

Parr, Adrian. *Birth of a New Earth: The Radical Politics of Environmentalism.* New York: Columbia University Press, 2017.

Payne, Charles M. *I've Got the Light of Freedom: The Organizing Tradition and the Mississippi Freedom Struggle.* Berkeley: University of California Press, 2007.

Philpott, Tom. "Joel Salatin's Unsustainable Myth." *Mother Jones.* November 19, 2020. https://www.motherjones.com/food/2020/11/joel-salatin -chris-newman-farming-rotational-grazing-agriculture/.

Phulwani, Vijay. "A Splendid Failure? Black Reconstruction and Du Bois's Tragic Vision of Politics." In *A Political Companion to W. E. B. DuBois,* ed. Nicholas Bromell, 271–302. Lexington: University of Kentucky Press, 2018.

Povinelli, Elizabeth A. *Between Gaia and Ground: Four Axioms of Existence and the Ancestral Catastrophe of Late Liberalism.* Durham, NC: Duke University Press, 2021.

——. *Geontologies: A Requiem to Late Liberalism.* Durham, NC: Duke University Press, 2016.

Polletta, Francesca. *Freedom Is an Endless Meeting.* Chicago: University of Chicago Press, 2004.

Reo, Nicholas James, and Kyle Whyte. "Hunting and Morality as Elements of Traditional Ecological Knowledge." *Human Ecology.* December 2010. http://dx.doi.org/10.2139/ssrn.1739805.

Roane, J. T. *Dark Agoras: Insurgent Black Social Life and the Politics of Place.* New York: New York University Press, 2023.

Roberts, Neil. *Freedom as Marronage.* Chicago: University of Chicago Press, 2015.

Robinson, Cedric. *Terms of Order: Political Science and the Myth of Leadership.* Chapel Hill: University of North Carolina Press, 2016.

Rogin, Michael. *Fathers and Children: Andrew Jackson and the Subjugation of the American Indian.* New York: Routledge, 1991.

Rose, Deborah Bird. *Reports from a Wild Country.* Randwick: University of New South Wales Press, 2004.

——. *Shimmer: Flying Fox Exuberance in Worlds of Peril.* Edinburgh: University of Edinburgh Press, 2022.

Rosivach, Vincent J. "Autochthony and the Athenians." *Classical Quarterly* 37, no. 2 (1987): 294–306.

Rowland, Susan. *Jung: A Feminist Revision.* London: Polity, 2002.

Roy, James. "Autochthony in Ancient Greece." In *A Companion to Ethnicity in the Ancient Mediterranean*, ed. Jeremy McInterney, 241–255. Hoboken, NJ: Wiley, 2014.

Sandel, Michael. *Democracy's Discontent*. Cambridge, MA: Harvard University Press, 2022.

Schlosberg, David. *Defining Environmental Justice*. Oxford: Oxford University Press, 2007.

Schlosberg, David, and Romand Coles. "The New Environmentalism of Everyday Life: Sustainability, Material Flows, and Movements." *Contemporary Political Theory* 15, no. 2 (2016): 160–181.

Schlosser, Joel Alden. *Herodotus in the Anthropocene*. Chicago: University of Chicago Press, 2020.

——. "Speaking Silence: Holding and the Democratic Arts of Mourning." In *The Democratic Arts of Mourning*, ed. A. Hirsch and D. McIvor, 187–205. Lanham, MD: Lexington Books, 2019.

Schmitt, Carl. *The Nomos of the Earth in the International Law of the Jus "Publicum Europaeum."* Candor, NY: G. L. Ulmen, 2006.

Schneider, Nathan. *Everything for Everyone: The Radical Tradition That Is Shaping the Next Economy*. New York: Nation Books, 2018.

Scott, James C. *Against the Grain*. New Haven, CT: Yale University Press, 2017.

——. *The Art of Not Being Governed*. New Haven, CT: Yale University Press, 2010.

——. *Domination and the Arts of Resistance*. New Haven, CT: Yale University Press, 1992.

——. *Seeing Like a State*. New Haven, CT: Yale University Press, 1998.

Sedgwick, Eve. *Touching Feeling: Affect, Pedagogy, Performativity*. Durham, NC: Duke University Press, 2002.

Sheldrake, Merlin. *Entangled Life: How Fungi Make Our Worlds, Change Our Minds, and Change Our Futures*. New York: Random House, 2021.

Sheldrake, Rupert. "The Extended Mind." *Quest*, July–August 2003, 1–6.

——. *The Presence of the Past: Morphic Resonance and the Memory of Nature*. Toronto: Park Street Press, 2012.

Simpson, Audra. *Mohawk Interruptus: Political Life Across the Borders of the Settler States*. Durham, NC: Duke University Press, 2014.

Simpson, Leanne Betasamosake. *As We Have Always Done*. Minneapolis: University of Minnesota Press, 2021.

———. "Land as pedagogy: Nishnaabeg Intelligence and Rebellious Transformation." *Decolonization: Indigeneity, Education and Society* 3, no. 3 (2014): 1–25.

———. *Dancing on Our Turtle's Back*. Winnipeg: Arbeiter Ring, 2011.

———. *The Gift Is in the Making*. Winnipeg: Portage and Main Press, 2013.

Spemann, H. *Embryonic Development and Induction*. New Haven, CT: Yale University Press, 1938.

Stout, Jeffrey. *Blessed Are the Organized: Grassroots Democracy in America*. Princeton, NJ: Princeton University Press, 2010.

Taylor, Charles. *The Ethics of Authenticity*. Cambridge, MA: Harvard University Press, 1992.

Thornton, Thomas F. *Being and Place Among the Tlingit*. Seattle: University of Washington Press, 2008.

Todd, Zoe. "Fish Pluralities: Human-Animal Relations and Sites of Engagement in Paulatuuq, Arctic Canada," *Études/Inuit/Studies* 38, nos. 1–2 (2014): 217–238.

Tsing, Anna Lowenhaupt. "The Sociality of Birds." In *Kin: Thinking with Deborah Bird Rose*, ed. Thom van Dooren and Matthew Chrulew, 15–32. Durham, NC: Duke University Press, 2022.

Tully, James. "Reconciliation Here on Earth." In *Resurgence and Reconciliation: Indigenous-Settler Relations and Earth Teachings*, ed. Michael Asch, John Borrows, and James Tully, 83–129. Toronto: University of Toronto Press, 2018.

———. *Strange Multiplicity: Constitutionalism in the Age of Diversity*. Cambridge: Cambridge University Press, 1995.

Van Dooren, Thom. *Flight Ways: Life and Loss at the Edge of Distinction*. New York: Columbia University Press, 2014.

Van Dooren, Thom, Eben Kirksey, and Ursula Münster. "Multispecies Studies: Cultivating Arts of Attentiveness." *Environmental Humanities* 8, no. 1 (2016): 1–23.

Viveiros de Castro, Eduardo. *The Relative Native: Essays on Indigenous Conceptual Worlds*. Chicago: HAU Press, 2015.

Vizenor, Gerald. *Manifest Manners: Narratives on Postindian Survivance*. Lincoln: University of Nebraska Press, 1999.

Warren, Mark R. *Dry Bones Rattling: Community Building to Revitalize American Democracy*. Princeton, NJ: Princeton University Press, 2001.

Wehr, Demaris. *Jung and Feminism: Liberating Archetypes*. London: Routledge, 1987.

Weiss, P. A. "Morphodynamische Feldtheorie und Genetik." *Zeitschrift für induktive Abstammungs- und Vererbungslehre* 2 (supplement) (1928): 1567–1574.

West, Paige. *Conservation Is Our Government Now: The Politics of Ecology in Papua New Guinea.* Durham, NC: Duke University Press, 2006.

———. *Dispossession and the Environment: Rhetoric and Inequality in Papua New Guinea.* New York: Columbia University Press, 2016.

Whitebook, Joel. *Perversion and Utopia.* Cambridge, MA: MIT Press, 1996.

Winnicott, D. W. *The Maturational Processes and the Facilitating Environment: Studies in the Theory of Emotional Development.* London: Karnac and the Institute of Psychoanalysis, 1990.

Wissler, Clark. *Mythology of the Blackfoot Indians.* Vol. 2, Pt. 1. New York: American Museum of Natural History, 1908.

Wolin, Sheldon S. "Democracy, Difference, and Recognition." *Political Theory* 21, no. 3 (1993): 464–483.

———. *Democracy, Incorporated: Managed Democracy and the Specter of Inverted Totalitarianism.* Princeton, NJ: Princeton University Press, 2008.

———. "Fugitive Democracy." *Constellations* 1 (1994): 11–25.

———. "Norm and Form: The Constitutionalizing of Democracy." In *Athenian Political Thought and the Reconstruction of American Democracy,* ed. J. Peter Euben, John R. Wallach, and Josiah Ober, 29–58. Ithaca, NY: Cornell University Press, 1994.

———. *Politics and Vision.* Exp. ed. Princeton, NJ: Princeton University Press, 2004.

———. *The Presence of the Past: Essays on the State and the Constitution.* Baltimore: John Hopkins University Press, 1989.

Woodly, Deva R. *Reckoning: Black Lives Matter and the Democratic Necessity of Social Movements.* New York: Oxford University Press, 2021.

Wynter, Silvia. "1492: A New World View." In *Race, Discourse, and the Origin of the Americas,* ed. Vera Lawrence Hyatt and Rex Nettleford, 5–57. Washington, DC: Smithsonian Institution Press, 1995.

Young, Iris Marion. *Inclusion and Democracy.* Oxford: Oxford University Press, 2002.

INDEX

Abram, David, 73–74, 105–106, 108–109
Adorno, Theodor, 70
Aeschylus, 169n33
agriculture, 35, 37–39, 87; carbon-intensive, 152; cooperative, 138; regenerative, 152, 157. *See also* play farming
Ahmed, Sabeen, 171n43
Alexander, Jeffrey C., 184n4
Allen, Amy, 71–72
Akuno, Kali, 137, 139. *See also* Cooperation Jackson
Americas, premodern, 39, 41–44
Anker, Elisabeth R., 165n3
Anishnaabe people, 153
anthropocentrism, 46, 49; and freedom, 50; and membership criteria, 90; and modern myths, 4, 28, 65–66; and political rituals, 145, 151

Anthropocene, 9, 11. *See also* Chthulucene
anthropology, 20, 37–38, 59; multispecies anthropology, 166n9; philosophical anthropology, 82
anxiety, 1–2, 166n4, 172n53
Anzaldúa, Gloria E., 16–17, 155
Apostolidis, Paul, 121n191
archetypes: anti-democratic, 102–103; archetypal patterns, 5, 65–66; archetypal resonance, 67, 78, 133, 143; and collective unconscious, 65, 74–85, 99, 101; criticisms of, 78–79; democratic, 20, 73, 85–104, 124; and earthborn(e) democracy, 5, 20, 731, 110–101; and the earthborn(e) unconscious, 104–108; and emancipation, 102; Guattari on, 84; Jungian, 20, 72, 74–80,

166n9, 167n12, 168n15; democracy and, 11, 17, 85; and freedom, 19, 59, 67; and Indigenous thought, 27, 48–58; Krenak on, 167n11; modern estrangement from, 72; and morphic resonance, 34; play and rootedness in, 59; reciprocal, 26, 62; rituals of, 21–22, 111, 113–160; and sovereignty, 168n23; spiritual dimension of, 60. *See also* Jung, Carl; multispecies entanglement

earthly flourishing, 16, 19, 21–22, 27–28, 36–37, 46–48, 50, 53, 56, 63, 66, 159, 169n29

earthly inheritance, 20, 22, 27, 36, 72, 118, 124, 142, 153, 160

Eastern Woodlands, 39

ecological crisis, 2–3, 23, 49, 70, 166n4

ecological holding environment, 36

eels, 132–134, 186

Eliade, Mircea, 64–65, 119

emergence, attunement and, 5, 117, 120, 122, 125, 126, 140, 143; archetypes and, 78, 85, 111, 150; as flight, 130; limits on, 88; morphic fields, 99, 123; resurgence, 128–129; rituals and, 21, 124, 133, 151, 153; visionary political theory and, 17–18

Enlightenment ideals, 70

entangled agency, 5, 21. *See also* distributed agency

entangled life. *See* earthly entanglement

entanglement. *See* earthly entanglement

Episcopal Church, 182n100

Erechtheus, 13

Escobar, Arturo, 166n9

Espejo, Paulina Ochoa, 185n23

Europe: culture and civilization, 78, 105; Enlightenment values of, 42; Indigenous critique of, 43; as origin of modernity, 41

extinction, sixth mass, 2, 70

fantasies: ancient Athens as democratic, 13; of political founding, 83; modern variety of, 2; role in orienting collective life, 70. *See also* myths

Farneth, Molly, 121–122

Federici, Silvia, 166n8; on commoning, 118; on re-enchanting the world, 113, 125

festivals, 123. *See also* rituals

flight (archetype), 73, 100; anti-democratic shadow of, 102–103; desire and, 83; as freedom of movement, freedom to disobey, and freedom to transform, 43, 87–88; generative refusal, 126; imaginative, 85, 89; into rather than from, 130–131; nonhuman practice, 132, 134; refuse "democracy" language, 10; relationship to sociality, 15; as return and renewal, 110, 158; as return of repressed, 90; rituals, 117; spiritual activism as, 155. See also *As We Have Always Done* (Simpson)

Flynn, James, 32